Ask a Question
HOW THINGS WORK

ARMADILLO

This paperback edition printed in 2009

© 1997 Bookmart Limited

ISBN: 978-1-84322-713-7

1 3 5 7 9 10 8 6 4 2

Published by Armadillo Books, an imprint of
Bookmart Limited, Registered Number 2372865
Trading as Bookmart Limited, Blaby Road,
Wigston, Leicestershire, LE18 4SE, England

Text: Nicola Baxter
Design: Amanda Hawkes
Cover Design: Anthony Prudente
Editorial Consultant: Ronne Randall

Originally published in 1998 as part of
1000 Questions & Answers

Printed in Thailand

CONTENTS

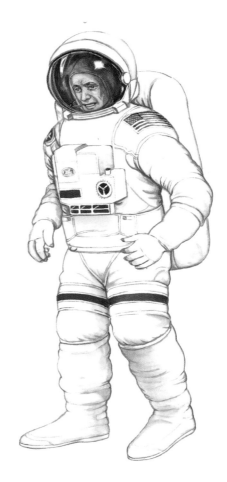

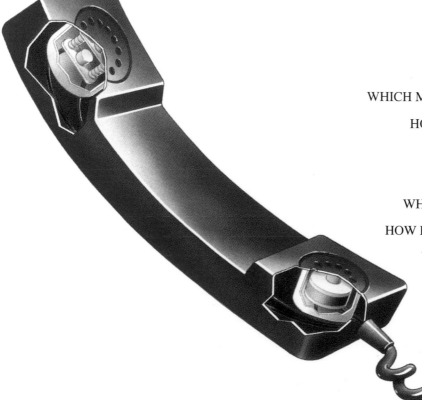

WHAT ARE THE SYSTEMS OF THE HUMAN BODY?

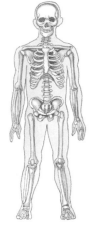

The central nervous system includes the brain and the nerves that carry messages to and from it.

Our bodies are very complicated. It is impossible to think about all the processes that are going on inside them at the same time, so doctors often consider the body as being made up of several different systems, each one with different organs and mechanisms working together to perform particular functions.

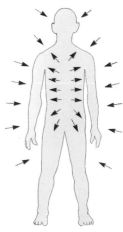

The immune system enables the body to fight off disease and illness and to remain healthy.

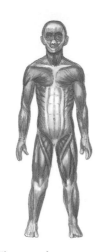

The skeletal system is the framework that supports and protects the soft parts of the body.

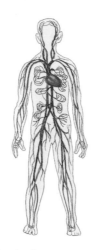

The muscular system enables the body to move. Muscles contract to cause movement.

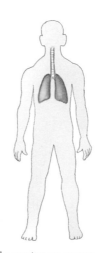

The circulatory system is concerned with the way in which blood flows around the body.

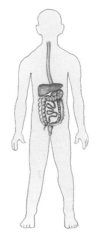

The respiratory system works to supply the body with the oxygen it needs from the air we breathe.

The digestive system enables us to absorb nutrients from what we eat and drink.

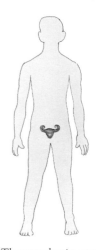

The reproductive system differs in males and females, allowing new humans to be born.

HOW DOES THE BRAIN WORK?

THERE IS MUCH that we do not yet know about how the brain works, but we do know that the brain communicates with the rest of the body through a thick cord of nerves running down the middle of the spine and branching off to reach the limbs and internal organs. The nerves are pathways for messages *to* the brain, to inform it about what is happening elsewhere in the body, and *from* the brain to tell the rest of the body how to act. These messages, and the processes happening within the brain, are made up of tiny electrical impulses. By far the largest part of the brain is the cerebrum, which is divided into two halves, called hemispheres. The rest of the brain is made up of the cerebellum, the pons and the medulla, which join together at the top of the spinal cord.

HOW MUCH FOOD DO WE NEED?

FOOD IS THE FUEL that our bodies need for movement. But we also need some fuel simply to maintain all the parts of our bodies. Individual cells are being renewed all the time. And even if we do not move the *outside* of our bodies at all, there are many parts *inside* that are constantly in motion. How much food we need depends on our size, age, gender and level of activity.

One very important function of the brain is memory, without which we would all be like tiny babies. Repetition seems to help the brain to memorize things. These dancers have probably repeated their actions over and over again.

Food energy is measured in kilojoules (kJ) or kilocalories (kcal). Until puberty, boys and girls need the same amount of food energy, but after that boys tend to need more. Of course, every person has different requirements, and a more active person will always require more food than an inactive one.

Boy or girl

Woman doing office work

Teenage girl

Teenage boy

Man doing office work

Man doing manual work

| 1000 kcal | 2000 kcal | 3000 kcal | 4000 kcal |
| 4200 kJ | 8400 kJ | 12,600 kJ | 16,800 kJ |

HOW MANY MUSCLES DO WE HAVE?

THERE ARE more than 600 muscles in the human body. Over 100 of these are in our faces, which is why we can have so many different expressions. Although we can perform a great variety of movements, each muscle can only do one thing: contract. That is why muscles often work in pairs, so that one muscle can move a part of the body in one direction, while its partner can move it back again. Perhaps the most important muscle in the human body is the heart, which is contracting and relaxing all the time to pump blood around the body.

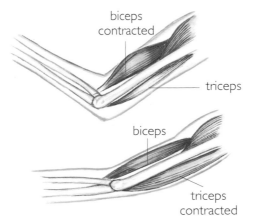

Two muscles work together in our upper arms. When the biceps muscle contracts, the forearm is lifted. When the triceps muscle contracts, the forearm is lowered again.

Once almost everyone did manual work of some kind. It was essential for survival. Human bodies were not designed for the sedentary lives many of us now lead. That is why exercise is important for good health.

HAVE HUMAN BODIES CHANGED THROUGH THE CENTURIES?

OVER MILLIONS OF YEARS, evolution is changing the way humans look. Over a shorter period, improved nutrition and medical discoveries have meant that people in some parts of the world today are generally bigger and stronger than their ancestors. But we are also losing some abilities that no longer seem useful. The smallest toe, for example, can no longer be moved independently by most people. As recently as Roman times, some people may have been able to "prick up their ears", moving them slightly towards sounds as some animals can.

WHAT IS THE DIFFERENCE BETWEEN VEINS AND ARTERIES?

VEINS ARE BLOOD VESSELS that carry blood to the heart, while arteries carry it from the heart. The heart acts as a pump, pushing blood to every part of the body. Adults have between five and six litres (between nine and ten pints) of blood. As well as containing red cells to carry oxygen to the body's organs, blood also plays an important part in fighting infection. White blood cells attack and digest harmful bacteria, while platelets in the blood form clots so that wounds can heal and no further infection can enter the body.

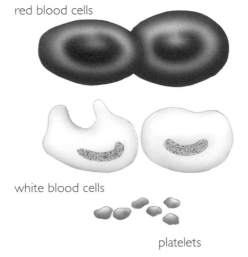

The three kinds of blood cell are carried in a yellowish liquid called plasma. Plasma is 90% water.

fast facts

WHICH IS THE LARGEST HUMAN CELL?

The largest human cell is the female egg cell. It is just visible as a tiny dot to the naked eye.

WHICH IS THE SMALLEST HUMAN CELL?

Strangely, the smallest human cell is the male sperm cell, which can fertilize an egg to create an embryo.

WHAT ARE HORMONES?

Hormones are substances made in glands that travel through the bloodstream to trigger various actions in different parts of the body. We create over 50 different hormones, such as insulin.

DO BABIES HAVE FEWER BONES THAN ADULTS?

In fact, babies have *more* bones than adults. Some bones in babies, such as in their skulls, hands and feet, are in separate parts when they are born and only fuse together later, as the baby grows.

HOW MANY TEETH DO HUMANS HAVE?

Humans usually have two sets of teeth. As babies, they grow 20 first teeth, often called milk teeth. Later, these fall out and a second set of 32 adult teeth grows, although the last four of these, called wisdom teeth, may not appear until a person is 18 or older, and sometimes do not grow at all.

WHY IS SMOKING BAD FOR HEALTH?

Your lungs have over 350 million tiny air sacs, called alveoli, in which oxygen is taken from the air and passed into your blood. Smoking coats these sacs with sticky tar, so that they cannot do their job.

WHICH IS THE MOST WIDELY SPOKEN LANGUAGE?

Languages are living things, changing all the time to meet the needs of their speakers and writers. It is only in the last few hundred years that attempts have been made to standardize the way in which languages are used, so that people using the same language can understand each other as well as possible. In the world today, Mandarin Chinese is the most widely used language, with over a billion speakers. English is next, with around half a billion speakers.

Chinese characters can be very complicated, with up to 26 strokes in each. The Japanese have adapted over two thousand characters to write their language, but they also have two alphabets, one for Japanese words and one for foreign words!

Perhaps the nearest thing we have to a universal language is road signs!

DO ALL LANGUAGES HAVE ALPHABETS?

ALPHABETS consist of letters that represent sounds. By writing different combinations of letters, all the sounds in a language can be represented. The first alphabet was probably developed by the Phoenicians before 1500BC. Even if they use the same letter forms, not all languages have the same number of letters in their alphabets. English, for example, uses 26 letters to write all its sounds, but Italian uses just 21, with j, k, w, x and y seen only in foreign words. However, the most widely spoken language of all, Chinese, does not use an alphabet. Instead, it has over 50,000 characters, each representing a word or part of a word.

ARE ALL LANGUAGES RELATED?

NOT ALL LANGUAGES are related, but they do seem to form related groups. Most languages that were originally European, some of which are now spoken all over the world, are thought to have developed from an ancient and unknown language that linguists know as "Proto Indo-European".

IS THERE A UNIVERSAL LANGUAGE?

MANY PEOPLE have dreamed of a world in which everyone speaks the same language. Some international jobs use one language to avoid dangerous misunderstandings. However, even gestures can be misunderstood, as a shake of the head can mean "yes" in some countries and "no" in others!

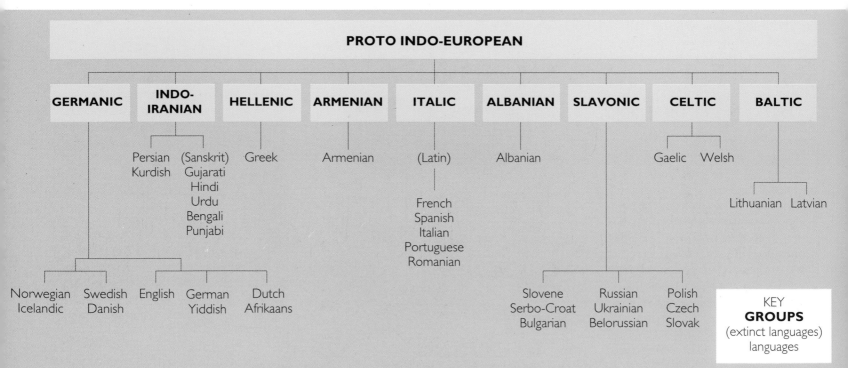

PROTO INDO-EUROPEAN

GERMANIC	INDO-IRANIAN	HELLENIC	ARMENIAN	ITALIC	ALBANIAN	SLAVONIC	CELTIC	BALTIC

Persian Kurdish — (Sanskrit) Gujarati Hindi Urdu Bengali Punjabi — Greek — Armenian — (Latin) — Albanian — Gaelic Welsh

French Spanish Italian Portuguese Romanian

Lithuanian Latvian

Norwegian Icelandic — Swedish Danish — English — German Yiddish — Dutch Afrikaans

Slovene Serbo-Croat Bulgarian — Russian Ukrainian Belorussian — Polish Czech Slovak

KEY
GROUPS
(extinct languages)
languages

HOW AND WHY ARE NEW WORDS INVENTED?

LANGUAGES grow and change because they need to. New words are invented when new ideas or articles require a name. Usually, new words are based on earlier ones. When the television was invented, the word chosen to describe it was a combination of an ancient Greek word, meaning "far" and a Latin word to do with "seeing". Sometimes a writer takes delight in inventing words. Lewis Carroll wrote a poem about a creature he called the "Jabberwock", for example.

WHAT IS THE ROSETTA STONE?

THIS STONE was found near Rosetta, in Egypt. On it was an inscription, given three times in three different languages. One of the versions was in Greek, which scholars could read. Another version was in ancient Egyptian hieroglyphs, a kind of picture-writing that no one in modern times had been able to decipher. Given the Greek "key", it became possible to read the hieroglyphs on the stone, and later, thousands of other hieroglyphs carved on monuments and buildings.

Sometimes a "new" word is simply borrowed from another language. "Chocolate" came into the English language as a version of the word that the Aztecs used to describe a drink made from the cocoa bean. This drink was unknown in Europe until the Spaniards discovered the Aztecs in South America. Once it was known, it had to be named! Borrowing the local name for it was an easy solution.

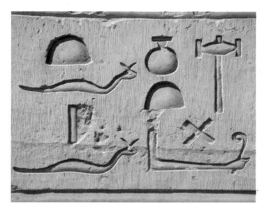

Until Egyptian hieroglyphs were deciphered, it was not known that most of them represent sounds and syllables, not whole words.

WHEN WAS BRAILLE DEVELOPED?

BRAILLE is a system of writing that uses raised dots, punched into paper or plastic. It enables people with little or no vision to read with their fingers. The system was invented in the first half of the nineteenth century by Louis Braille (1809–52), a Frenchman who had himself been blind since the age of three.

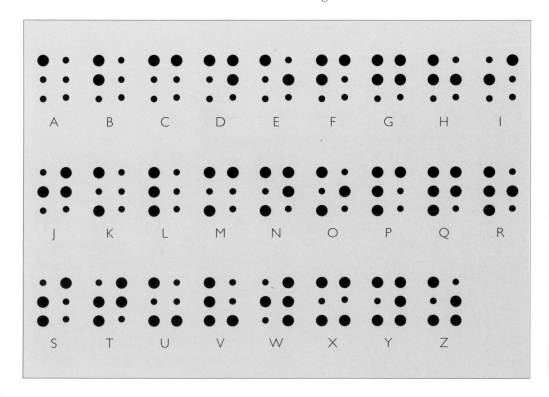

A B C D E F G H I

J K L M N O P Q R

S T U V W X Y Z

fast facts

WHAT IS A DIALECT?

A language may have speakers who use different accents, vocabularies and ways of putting words together. Varying forms of the same language are called dialects, especially when they are found in particular regions.

WHICH ARE THE RAREST LANGUAGES?

Usually, when the last person to speak a language dies, the language dies too, even if it has been recorded. Each year, a few languages or dialects disappear for ever. This is specially true at the moment of some native American languages.

CAN ANYONE SPEAK ANY LANGUAGE?

Babies are born with the ability to make the sounds of any language, but as they learn one language, they gradually lose this ability.

WHAT IS ESPERANTO?

Esperanto is a language invented in 1887 by a Polish doctor called Zamenhof. He hoped that it would become a worldwide language.

HOW SOON DO CHILDREN RECOGNIZE THEIR NATIVE LANGUAGE?

Researchers have found that children as young as three months can tell the difference between the language they hear most frequently and other languages or even dialects.

HOW CAN WE TELL HOW ANCIENT LANGUAGES WERE PRONOUNCED?

We cannot be sure how languages of long ago sounded. However, by studying how languages change over time and looking at poetry in the dead languages, it may be possible to make a good guess about how they sounded.

HOW HAVE MODERN COMMUNICATIONS CHANGED OUR LIVES?

Modern communications have affected our lives in numerous ways. Being able to pass information down telephone wires or via satellites means that some people can work from anywhere in the world and still keep in constant touch with their offices. A surgeon in Arizona, via a satellite link, can assist a colleague in Beijing with a complicated operation. News can travel halfway around the world as quickly as it can reach the next town. Perhaps the biggest effect of communications has been to make us all feel that the world is a smaller place, and that we need to be concerned about its future and the futures of people thousands of miles away.

Communication satellites usually circle the Earth in what is called a geostationary orbit. This means that the satellite is always above the same point on the Earth's surface.

HOW MUCH HAS THE SPEED OF COMMUNICATION INCREASED?

ONLY A FEW HUNDRED YEARS ago, the fastest way that a piece of news could travel was to be carried by a person on horseback. Messages sent overseas could only travel as fast as the fastest sailing ship and were at the mercy of the wind and weather. The development of steam locomotives and steamships made it possible for information to move around the world more quickly, but it still had to travel physically from one place to another, as a letter. The breakthrough came with the invention of the electric telegraph and messages in Morse Code. The message was sent down a wire in bursts of electric current. Today, images of written documents, sound recordings or television pictures can be flashed around the globe in less than a second by means of satellites and radio communications.

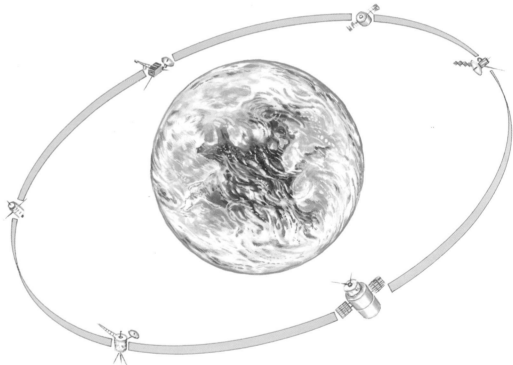

Satellites have different shapes and sizes, depending on the job they have to do. They are launched into orbit around the Earth by rockets. As a result, they are very expensive to put into position. Astronauts are sometimes sent to repair damaged satellites.

HOW DO COMMUNICATION SATELLITES WORK?

THE LAYER of the Earth's atmosphere called the ionosphere can reflect some radio waves back to Earth. This is used for sending messages over fairly short distances, but for messages to travel further across the Earth, the radio signals can be bounced off a satellite, orbiting almost 36,000km (22,000 miles) above the Earth's surface. Several satellites, in different orbits, are required to give coverage over the whole globe, and different satellites are used to reflect signals for different media, such as telephone messages and television pictures.

WHAT IS SEMAPHORE?

SEMAPHORE is a means of signalling using pairs of flags. Different flag positions stand for different letters and numbers. Semaphore signals are useful when the signaller is within sight of the receiver of the message but too far away to call out. It was widely used between ships sailing near each other in the days before ship-to-ship radio.

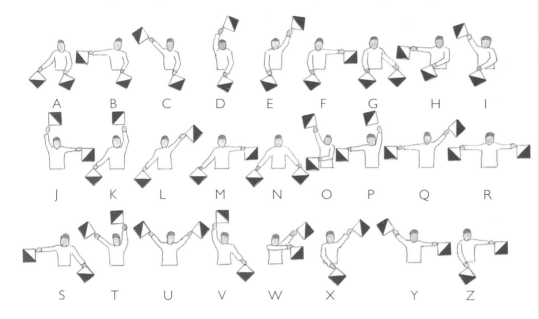

HOW DOES A TELEPHONE WORK?

A TELEPHONE works by sending and receiving electrical signals that represent sounds, including the human voice. When the required number is dialled, a signal passes to the called telephone, causing it to ring, buzz, flash a light, or even vibrate to attract the attention of the person using it. When the telephone is picked up or switched on, a connection is made, and a conversation can take place.

The receiver of the telephone converts the electric current back into sounds by using an electromagnet to make a diaphragm vibrate.

The mouthpiece contains a microphone. Sound vibrations are converted into an electric current which varies as the sounds do.

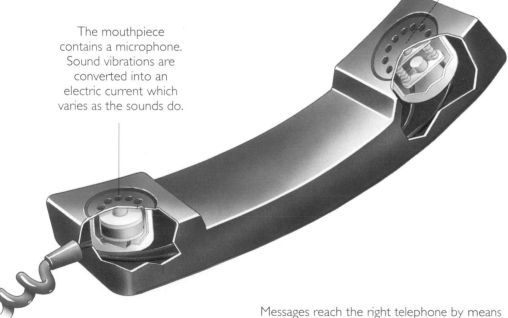

Telephone messages can travel as electrical signals along wires or through the air as radio waves. As signals take time to travel, you may notice a very slight delay in the response of the person being called if they are thousands of miles away.

Messages reach the right telephone by means of a dialled number. Pressing the keys of the telephone causes different electrical pulses or varying tones to pass to electronic equipment at the telephone exchange. This "reads" the pulses or tones and routes the call to the correct area and telephone.

WHAT IS E-MAIL?

E-mail is short for "electronic mail". It is a way of sending messages between computers along telephone wires or using radio signals.

HOW WILL COMMUNICATIONS IMPROVE IN THE FUTURE?

In the future it is likely that each one of us will be able to carry a full communications system with us, as telephones, computers and even television screens become smaller and smaller.

WHAT IS AN OPTICAL FIBRE?

An optical fibre is made of fine strands of glass, along which pulses of light can travel. Optical fibres are used to carry signals, such as telephone messages. Each optical fibre can carry thousands of telephone messages at the same time.

WHEN WAS THE TELEPHONE INVENTED?

The invention of the telephone is often attributed to Alexander Graham Bell (1847–1922), a Scottish-American inventor who patented a practical telephone in 1876. As is often the case, other inventors had already proposed similar machines.

HOW DOES A FAX MACHINE WORK?

"Fax" is a short way of saying "facsimile", meaning an exact copy of a document. A fax machine scans each tiny section of a document and sends signals by telephone wires or radio waves to another fax machine, communicating whether the section is light or dark. The receiving machine converts these signals back into light and dark sections on light-sensitive paper, or prints them onto plain paper.

WHY DO SHIPS FLOAT?

force of gravity pulling
the ship downwards

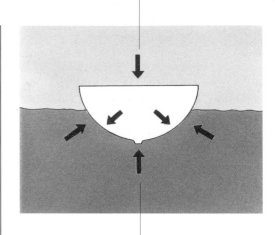

upward force of the displaced water

Ships float, even if they are made of iron, because their overall density is less than that of the water that supports them. The water displaced (pushed aside) by the hull of the ship pushes back upwards with a force called upthrust or buoyancy. If this is equal to or greater than the force of gravity pulling the ship's mass downwards, the vessel will float. In fact, ships need a certain amount of weight to give them stability in the water, so many of them have hulls weighted with concrete or another kind of ballast. Without it, the ship would bob around on the water like a cork.

ARE SHIPS STILL IMPORTANT NOW THAT AIR, ROAD AND RAIL TRAVEL ARE SO MUCH FASTER?

SHIPS are of vital importance to the world's economy. They carry over 90% of the freight that travels around the globe. Although air travel is a quicker way of crossing the oceans, it is very expensive, and weight is always a problem. Ships may be slower, but they can carry enormous loads. Nowadays many loads are carried in large steel containers, which can be stacked on the ship and then lifted by crane directly onto the back of a truck in the port, doing away with the need to pack and unpack cargo at each change of carrier.

Containers protect the goods inside. They can be stored in stacks on the dockside until transferred to a ship, truck or train.

HOW DOES A SUBMARINE SUBMERGE AND SURFACE?

SUBMARINES, unlike most ships, are not always required to float! In order to make a submarine sink beneath the surface, its density must be increased to be greater than that of the water. This is done by taking in water, which fills ballast tanks within the outer hull of the submarine. The amount of water entering can be controlled, so that the vessel sinks slowly. To bring a submarine back to the surface, pumps force the water out of ballast tanks. The submarine's density becomes less than that of the water it is displacing, so it rises.

Water fills the ballast tanks, causing the submarine to sink.

When water is pumped out of the ballast tanks, the submarine rises.

WHAT IS A PERISCOPE?

A PERISCOPE is a metal tube that can be extended above the submarine while it is underwater. The tube contains lenses and mirrors, which enable an image of the scene above the surface to be seen below in the submarine. The periscope can swivel, so that a 360° view is obtained.

The operator turns the periscope by means of the handles on the side. These fold up when it is not in use, as space is always at a premium in a submarine.

WHY ARE PORT AND STARBOARD SO CALLED?

TRADITIONALLY, the lefthand side of a ship, looking forward, is called the port side, while the righthand side is called the starboard side. The term "starboard" comes from "steerboard". The large oar used to steer early ships was usually on the right. "Port" comes from the fact that ships had to tie up on the left side in port so that their steering oar would not be crushed against the dock.

At night, ships show a green light on their starboard side and a red light on their port side.

In a race, it is often the efficiency with which a boat tacks, compared with its competitors, that makes it a winner.

HOW DOES A YACHT TACK?

SAILORS cannot change the direction of the wind, but they are not powerless to change the direction of their sailing boats. By steering a zigzag course, called tacking, they are able to sail in the direction they require. This can be a time-consuming process. It is important that the navigator keeps an accurate check on the boat's position, so that it does not travel too far off course while tacking.

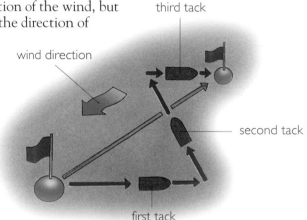

third tack

wind direction

second tack

first tack

WHAT WERE THE FIRST BOATS LIKE?

IT IS LIKELY that the first boats were made of hollowed-out tree trunks. Perhaps early humans saw fallen hollow logs floating along a river and realized that they could carry goods and people. Tree trunks were hollowed using stone axes and fire. A dugout pine canoe, found in the Netherlands, is thought to be at least 8000 years old.

fast facts

WHAT HAPPENED TO THE MARIE CELESTE?

The *Marie Celeste* was a sailing ship, found floating at sea in 1872. The sailors who found the ship claimed that everything was in its place, with an untouched dinner on the captain's table. Many suggestions have been made as to the fate of the ten crew, but the likeliest explanation is that the sailors who discovered the ship exaggerated in the stories they told, ignoring signs of pirate attack or illness.

WHAT WAS A TRIREME?

A trireme was an ancient Greek warship, powered by three rows of rowers, positioned above each other on both sides of the ship. The oars of the upper rows needed to be longer than the lower ones to reach the water.

WHAT IS A PLIMSOLL LINE?

A Plimsoll Line, named after the man who proposed it in 1876, is a line or series of lines on the side of a ship, marking the highest safe water level in various conditions. It ensures that merchant vessels are not overloaded.

WHY ARE SHIPS OFTEN REFERRED TO AS "SHE"?

One reason for ships being thought of as female may date from the days when, during a voyage that might take months or even years, male sailors came to think of the ship as home, supplying all they had of comfort and security. In this way, the ship was like the mothers and wives that the men had left in their homes on shore.

WHICH WAS THE FIRST CAR?

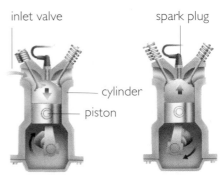

inlet valve   spark plug

cylinder

piston

The very first vehicle able to run on the open road was powered by steam. It was a three-wheeled tractor, built in 1769 by a Frenchman, Nicolas Cugnot (1725–1804). However, it was not until the development of the internal combustion engine in the second half of the nineteenth century that motor transport began to be successful. Both Gottlieb Daimler (1834–1900) and Karl Benz (1844–1929) were working on such engines in the 1880s in Germany. It is said that neither knew about the other's work, although they lived less than 100km apart.

1. As the piston moves down, it sucks air and fuel into the cylinder.

3. A spark from the spark plug makes the fuel burn. This causes the gases to expand and push the piston down.

HOW DOES THE INTERNAL COMBUSTION ENGINE WORK?

INTERNAL COMBUSTION ENGINES are usually fuelled by petrol or diesel. This fuel is burnt (combusted) within metal cylinders. The burning fuel causes a piston to move up and down inside each cylinder, and it is this upward and downward movement that is translated into a turning movement by the crankshaft, causing the axles and wheels to turn and the car to move.

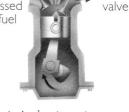

compressed air and fuel

exhaust valve

2. As the piston goes up, it compresses the air and fuel mixture, causing it to heat up.

4. As the piston rises again, exhaust gases are pushed out of the cylinder.

WHAT ARE THE MAIN SYSTEMS OF A CAR?

LIKE THE HUMAN BODY, a car can be thought of as having systems with different functions, all working together to make the vehicle operate effectively. The most important systems are shown in the illustration below.

Electrical system
As well as moving the wheels, the engine also powers an alternator, or dynamo, which generates electrical current. This current is stored in the battery. This supplies energy for the car's lights, windscreen wipers, radio and such features as electric windows.

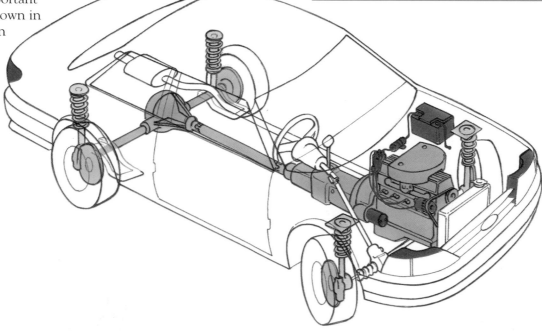

Suspension system
The suspension is a system of springs and shock absorbers that prevents every jolt caused by an uneven road surface being felt by the driver and passengers inside the car.

Transmission system
The transmission system consists of the crankshaft, gears and the differential. This is a system of gears on the axles that allows the wheels to travel at different speeds when going round corners, when the outer wheel travels further than the inner one.

Braking system
Each wheel has a brake unit, connected to the brake pedal by a tube full of brake fluid. Pushing the pedal forces the fluid down the tube, causing a brake shoe to press against a metal disk or drum on the inside of the wheel. Friction causes the wheels to slow and stop.

WHAT IS A CUSTOM CAR?

A CUSTOM CAR is one that has been altered from the manufacturer's original specifications to suit the wishes of its owner. This may involve painting it with extraordinary designs, making the engine more powerful, or even "stretching" it by cutting the entire car in half and inserting additional body parts. Some cars have been made very long indeed by this method. The one below has 26 wheels and contains a swimming pool!

This car was designed by Jay Ohrberg of California, USA. It is over 30m (100ft) long.

HOW DO RACING CAR DRIVERS ACHIEVE HIGH SPEEDS?

FORMULA 1 drivers cannot win races by themselves. Large teams of mechanics and technicians are needed to enable the car to perform well. The driver spends more time testing the car than he does racing, and no aspect of the vehicle is ignored. Even while the car is waiting at the start of a race, special electric heaters are warming the tyres so that they give their best performance. Every second counts in motor racing, so mechanics practise until they can change all four tyres of the car in under three seconds! Controlling the car at high speed puts enormous physical and mental strain on the driver. There is no power steering in Formula 1 cars, so the driver needs great strength and split-second reactions.

Non-professional drivers enjoy competing at many levels of motor racing. Here the actor Paul Newman is preparing to practise for the Daytona 24-hour race.

WHAT IS THE DIFFERENCE BETWEEN A VETERAN CAR AND A VINTAGE CAR?

A VETERAN CAR was made between 1896 and 1903, while a vintage car was built after 1904 and before 1930.

This vintage car is an Austin 7 "Chummy" Tourer, built in 1923.

WHEN WERE SPEED LIMITS INTRODUCED?

Speed limits are almost as old as cars themselves. Early motor vehicles were thought to travel at a dangerous speed, so the first cars in Britain, for example, were required to have a man with a red flag walking in front of them, and had to observe a speed limit of less than 5 miles per hour!

WHAT WAS SPECIAL ABOUT THE MODEL T FORD?

The Model T Ford was the first car to be built on a moving production line. This made the manufacturing process much cheaper and put motor cars within reach of many more people. Henry Ford (1863–1947) began the mass-production of motor cars that continues today.

WHAT IS FOUR-WHEEL DRIVE?

In most modern cars, the engine drives the front wheels of the car. In rear-wheel drive cars, it turns the back axle. In four-wheel drive cars, both axles are driven by the engine, enabling the car to travel powerfully over rough ground.

HOW WILL MOTOR CARS CHANGE IN THE FUTURE?

TWO AREAS of car design have been researched very thoroughly in the past few years. One of these concerns fuel consumption and exhaust gases, as the realization grows that the world's fossil fuels are polluting the atmosphere. The other is safety. It is likely that future cars will be able to prevent some accidents by assessing the distance to an obstacle and taking evasive action without prompting from the driver.

Streamlining helps to save fuel by reducing air resistance. Modern cars tend to have rounded angles and door handles that are flush with the bodywork, as this Chrysler Showcar does.

WHICH WAS THE WORLD'S FIRST PUBLIC RAILWAY?

The first public railway in the world to run a regular service was opened on 27 September 1825. It ran between Stockton and Darlington in the north of England. A steam train called The Locomotion pulled 34 wagons, some of which carried coal, while others were adapted to carry passengers. Both the locomotive and its track were built to the design of George Stephenson (1781–1848). Stephenson's background was in mining engineering. Coal mines had long used tracks to move wagons of coal, and it was with steam engines for these wagons that Stephenson first experimented.

WHAT DO THE NUMBERS BEFORE STEAM TRAIN NAMES MEAN?

STEAM LOCOMOTIVES are described by the arrangement of their leading, driving and trailing wheels. In fact, only the driving wheels are connected to the cylinders that provide the engine's power. So a 2-8-2 has two leading wheels, eight driving wheels and two trailing wheels.

Steam trains are still running scheduled services in some parts of the world. This is a 2-6-2 engine in Sumatra.

WHO INVENTED THE LOCOMOTIVE?

A LOCOMOTIVE is an engine that can travel under its own power, not pulled by horses, for example. But we usually think of it as running on tracks, or tramways, as they were first called. In 1804, Richard Trevithick (1771–1833), an English inventor, designed a train to pull coal wagons in a Welsh colliery. Trevithick was convinced that steam engines had a great future and later travelled to Peru and Costa Rica, where he introduced steam engines into the silver mines.

ROCKET

In 1829, Stephenson built an engine called The Rocket, which won a competition of steam trains called the Rainhill Trials by running at 48km/h (30mph).

fast facts

WHAT WAS THE ORIENT EXPRESS?

Some special trains have gained a romantic image over the years. The Orient Express was a luxurious train running between Paris, France, and Istanbul, Turkey, from 1883. Today, the train still travels over part of this route.

WHAT IS THE LONGEST JOURNEY THAT CAN BE MADE BY TRAIN?

Without changing trains at any point, the longest journey that can be made is 9297km (5777 miles) between Moscow and Vladivostok on the Russian Trans-Siberian line.

WHEN DID RAILWAYS FIRST CROSS THE UNITED STATES?

Railways spread across the world very quickly. In the 1850s, settlers suffered hardship crossing the American continent in wagons. By 1869, the journey could be made by train in relative comfort.

WHAT IS A MONORAIL?

A monorail, as the word suggests, is a railway with only one rail, on which an electric train can run.

WHERE WAS THE FIRST UNDERGROUND RAILWAY BUILT?

THE WORLD'S FIRST city underground railway line was opened in 1863 in London. It was called the Metropolitan.

HOW ARE UNDERGROUND RAILWAYS BUILT UNDER EXISTING CITIES?

BENEATH CITIES are the foundations of large buildings and many pipes carrying water, electricity, gas and telephone cables. Builders have either to tunnel very deeply or to use a technique called "cut-and-cover", which means that they run the railway under existing roads, so that they simply have to dig a huge trench along the road, build the railway, and cover it up again.

WHAT IS THE GAUGE OF A RAILWAY?

THE GAUGE of a railway is the distance between its rails. At one time, the standard gauge in several countries was 1.48m (4ft 10.25in), which was thought to have been the width of Roman chariot tracks. Today, many different gauges are used.

WHAT IS A COWCATCHER?

A COWCATCHER is a V-shaped metal part on the front of a train, designed to push obstacles – including cows! – off the line before the wheels hit them. The American Denver and Rio Grande steam engine below has an example.

HOW DO TRAINS CHANGE TRACKS?

THE INTERSECTIONS that allow a train to move over onto another track are called switches or points. Short pieces of rail are able to move across to bridge the gap between the two tracks, so that the train's wheels cross over as smoothly as possible.

The TGV (Train à Grande Vitesse) of France (left) and the Bullet Train of Japan (below) are two of the fastest trains in the world, aiming to run at 300km/h (186mph) in regular service.

Underground railways help to ease surface congestion in cities around the world. The underground railway in Paris, France, is called the Metro, which is short for Metropolitan, the first underground railway.

HOW DO PLANES FLY?

Aeroplanes fly when two of the four forces acting upon them are greater than the other two. The force of thrust, created by the aeroplane's propellers or jet engines, moves the plane forward. The force of lift is caused by air flowing over the wings. This keeps the plane in the air. The two forces working against thrust and lift are gravity, which pulls the plane towards the Earth, and drag, caused by air resistance, which slows the plane's forward motion.

Although they cannot fly in very rough weather, helicopters are extremely useful for rescues at sea, as they can hover over the site of a wreck.

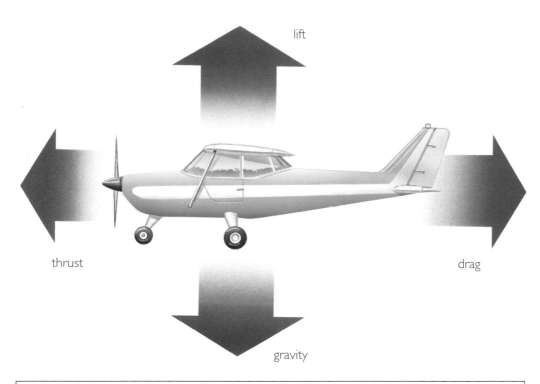

lift

thrust

drag

gravity

WHY IS A HELICOPTER SO MANOEUVRABLE?

HELICOPTERS have rotor blades above them that are aerofoils. When they turn rapidly, they create lift. The blades are tilted slightly, so that they also provide thrust. The helicopter's tail rotor blades stop the helicopter from spinning and enable it to turn. With this combination of rotors, a helicopter can move in any direction or simply hover. Without long wings, helicopters can manoeuvre in tight places, such as alongside cliff faces, so they are particularly useful for rescue and emergency work.

HOW DO AN AEROPLANE'S WINGS CREATE LIFT?

THE SHAPE of all parts of a plane is important, as the more streamlined it is, the less air resistance will cause drag to slow the plane. But the form of the wings is particularly important. The wings of most planes are shaped so that the upper surface is more curved than the lower surface. As the diagram shows, this affects the way in which air moves over them. The air travelling over the upper surface of the wing has further to travel and therefore moves faster than that passing under the wing. This creates an area of lower pressure above the wing, which sucks the wing upwards, creating the force of lift.

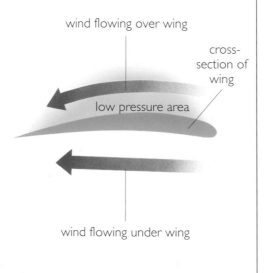

wind flowing over wing

cross-section of wing

low pressure area

wind flowing under wing

The shape of an aeroplane's wing is called an aerofoil.

HOW CAN GLIDERS FLY WITHOUT ENGINES?

GLIDERS are so light that the lift created by their wings can overcome the opposing pull of gravity. However, without engines, gliders cannot take off. There are two widely used methods of launching gliders into the air. They can be catapulted upwards from the ground, or they can be towed up by an aeroplane. The cable between the plane and the glider is then released, and the glider can fly solo. A glider flight is an extraordinary experience, as it is almost silent except for the sound of the wind.

HOW DO AIR TRAFFIC CONTROLLERS COMMUNICATE WITH PILOTS?

AIR TRAFFIC CONTROLLERS have screens on which they can see the planes in their sector. It is their job to see that planes are kept safely apart and guided appropriately during take-off and landing. When aeroplanes are near enough, the air traffic controllers can speak to them directly, but they cannot be expected to speak all the languages of international pilots. For this reason, to make communications as safe and clear as possible, all instructions and discussions take place in English all over the world.

Air traffic controllers use an aircraft's registration mark when calling it by radio. As one letter can sound rather like another, words are used instead, each one standing for the letter that begins it.

A Alpha	H Hotel	O Oscar	V Victor
B Bravo	I India	P Papa	W Whisky
C Charlie	J Juliet	Q Quebec	X X-Ray
D Delta	K Kilo	R Romeo	Y Yankee
E Echo	L Lima	S Sierra	Z Zulu
F Foxtrot	M Mike	T Tango	
G Golf	N November	U Uniform	

WHAT IS AN AIRSHIP?

AN AIRSHIP is a cigar-shaped balloon, filled with a gas. Nowadays, this is usually helium, as it cannot catch-fire, unlike the hydrogen used in earlier airships. Beneath the balloon, a cabin (often called a gondola) and engines are suspended. In the 1930s, the Germans developed airships called Zeppelins, although the tragic crash of the Hindenburg in the USA in 1937 really spelled the end of the age of the airship.

Today's airships are usually built for publicity purposes rather than as passenger carriers.

This is a 1939 Piper J-3 Cub, flying over Clear Lake, California, USA.

WHICH PLANES CAN LAND ON WATER?

SEAPLANES and flying boats have floats instead of wheels, so that they can land on water. In the 1930s, flying boats were often larger and more luxurious than ordinary aircraft, as they could be made larger without the expense of creating longer runways at airports around the world. Instead, they took off and landed at sea, taxiing in and out of existing harbours.

fast facts

WHICH PLANE CAN AVOID RADAR DETECTION?

Small planes may be able to avoid radar detection by flying very low, but the Northrop B2 Stealth bomber is made of special materials that can absorb radar, while its "flying wing" shape also helps it to avoid detection.

WHEN WAS THE FIRST AEROPLANE FLIGHT?

On 17 December 1903, Orville Wright took off in a plane called the Flyer and travelled 37m (121ft) – only just over half the length of a modern Boeing 747. Orville Wright had designed and built the plane with his brother Wilbur.

WHAT DOES A FLIGHT RECORDER RECORD?

A flight recorder is an electronic recording device contained in a waterproof and fireproof box. It records the plane's speed, height and direction, as well as the conversations of the crew with each other and with ground control. If the plane crashes, the flight recorder can give vital information that will help to save lives in the future.

HOW DO PLANES REFUEL WITHOUT LANDING?

Sometimes planes need to refuel in mid-air. Perhaps they are crossing an ocean or enemy territory. In this case, by very skilful manoeuvring, it is possible for another plane to transfer fuel through a flexible pipe. This is a difficult and potentially dangerous operation.

WHY DOES A ROCKET HAVE STAGES?

A rocket needs enormous power to escape from the Earth's gravity. The velocity required to achieve this is called the escape velocity, which is about 49,000km/h (29,000mph). The rocket's power comes from burning liquid hydrogen and oxygen. Each stage of a rocket is a fuel tank, which is jettisoned when its fuel is used up. After all, carrying an empty fuel tank will only use up more fuel. Only the top stage of the rocket, called the payload, makes the whole journey and brings the crew back to Earth.

A crew of up to eight people has to train for several months to become familiar with the controls in the shuttle's cockpit.

HOW CAN THE SPACE SHUTTLE BE USED OVER AND OVER AGAIN?

AT LIFT-OFF, the space shuttle has two rocket boosters. These are jettisoned when the shuttle reaches a height of 43km (27 miles). The shuttle usually remains in orbit around the Earth for about seven days, although it can continue for 30 days. When it returns to Earth, the shuttle lands on a runway, in a similar way to an ordinary aircraft. The rocket boosters are reattached to it, so that it is ready for another mission.

HOW DO ASTRONAUTS MOVE OUTSIDE THE SHUTTLE?

ASTRONAUTS outside the shuttle are encumbered by a heavy spacesuit, but this is not really a problem in weightless conditions. Controlled movement is more difficult, however. Astronauts wear a unit called a manned manoeuvring unit (MMU) on their backs. This is fuelled by nitrogen and is rechargeable in the shuttle. Several small thrusters allow the astronaut to move in all directions.

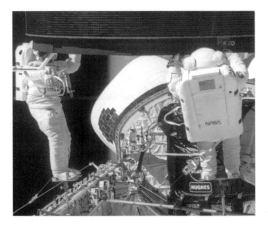

WHAT IS THE SPACE SHUTTLE USED FOR?

THE SPACE SHUTTLE has many uses and, because it is reusable, has made it possible to pursue some space activities that would otherwise have been too expensive. It is used to launch satellites and to make repairs to existing satellites. The shuttle can also be used as a laboratory, in which to carry out experiments that are only possible in zero gravity.

CAN ANY HUMAN STRUCTURE BE SEEN FROM SPACE?

THE GREAT WALL, which stretches for over 3640km (2150 miles) across China, is the only human structure that can be seen from space.

HOW DOES A SPACESUIT WORK?

A SPACESUIT is all that stands between an astronaut on a space walk and the emptiness of space. It must supply all his or her needs. There is no breathable atmosphere in space, so a spacesuit supplies oxygen to the astronaut.

Within the helmet, headphones and a microphone enable the astronaut to communicate with crew members and mission control.

A specially treated dark visor protects the astronaut's eyes from the glare of the Sun, while lights can illuminate dark areas.

A camera may be fixed to the astronaut's shoulder, so that other crew members and the ground crew can watch what is being done.

All the joins in the spacesuit must be absolutely airtight. Inside, the spacesuit is pressurized, like a deep-sea diver's suit.

The temperature, pressure and oxygen levels inside the suit are monitored by a control pack on the astronaut's front or back.

Under the outer suit, a body suit contains pipes through which cool liquid flows to protect the astronaut from the heat of the Sun.

The visor and outer layer of the spacesuit must be tough enough not to be torn or cracked by tiny meteorites that may bounce off the astronaut.

Suits are made of artificial materials that offer maximum protection, such as nylon, Kevlar and Dacron.

The astronaut is completely sealed within his or her suit, so urine is collected inside for disposal later!

On Earth, a spacesuit can be as difficult to walk in as a suit of armour, but in the weightlessness of space, the pull of gravity is not a consideration.

fast facts

HOW DO ASTRONAUTS SLEEP IN ZERO GRAVITY?

In order to prevent themselves floating around as they sleep, astronauts have to strap themselves down. Of course, it is important that everything else in the cabin is also firmly fixed.

WHO WAS THE FIRST PERSON IN SPACE?

The Russian cosmonaut Yuri Alekseyevich Gagarin was the first person to travel into space on 12 April 1961 in *Vostok 1*.

WHAT WAS THE SPACE RACE?

In the 1960s and 70s, both the USA and the USSR were investing considerable resources in space exploration at a time when tension between the two countries was high. Their endeavours to outdo each other in outer space were known as the space race. Today, Russian cosmonauts and American astronauts work together on international projects.

WHAT HAPPENS TO SPACE PROBES WHEN THEIR TASK IS DONE?

Most space probes are sent out with a particular job in mind, such as taking photographs or testing the atmosphere of a certain planet. But when this is done, those that have not landed on a planet's surface simply travel on through space. The American probe *Pioneer 10*, for example, sent to Jupiter on 2 March 1972, was still sending back signals from outside our Solar System 25 years later.

WHO WAS THE FIRST MAN ON THE MOON?

Neil Armstrong became the first man to step onto the Moon on 20 July 1969.

WHO WERE THE FIRST GREAT ROAD-BUILDERS?

From the earliest times, humans and animals have created track-ways along well-used routes, but it was the Romans who were the first to set about road-building in a systematic manner. The Roman Empire stretched from North Africa to Scotland. In order to govern successfully, the occupying forces needed to be able to reach trouble spots quickly. Roman roads were built so that armies could march rapidly for hundreds of miles.

Medieval bridges often used arches for support and had shops built along them to catch the passing trade of travellers who had no option but to cross the bridge.

An arch bridge uses the strength of an arch for support, although the roadway itself is usually straight.

A top level of paving stones gave a smooth surface for carts and marching armies.

Roman roads were made in layers. First the route was cleared of large stones and boulders. Then the bed of the road was levelled with sand.

The Romans tried to build straight roads as far as possible. Straight roads were easier to march along and reduced the risk of ambush, as the view was clear in both directions.

Rubble and crushed stone were rammed down on top of the sand.

Drainage ditches beside the road kept it dry.

A bascule bridge has two sections that can be opened so that shipping can pass through.

Suspension bridges have towers from which steel cables stretch to support the bridge beneath.

WHAT ARE THE DIFFERENT KINDS OF BRIDGES?

THE EARLIEST BRIDGES were probably tree trunks across streams or flat slabs of rock. Gradually, people learned to span wider rivers and ravines by supporting the bridge in the middle. Since then, engineers have devised ways of spanning very wide distances.

Beam bridges usually have fairly short spans. Today they are often supported by concrete piers.

WHEN WAS THE HEYDAY OF CANAL-BUILDING?

FOR THOUSANDS OF YEARS, people have transported heavy goods along waterways. The first canals were probably built to join existing navigable rivers. In the fifteenth century, the Aztec city of Tenochtitlan had a sophisticated series of canals, providing transport for goods and people. Venice, in Italy, although a smaller city, was also built on a system of canals rather than roads. However, the golden age of canal-building probably came with the Industrial Revolution, when there was an enormous need for cheap and easy ways to carry the goods made in factories to the nearest port. Canal boats, powered at first by a horse on the towpath and later by coal-fired steam engines, could carry enormous loads much more conveniently than horsedrawn carts on bumpy roads.

In England, barges and narrowboats were often brightly painted with patterns and scenes from life on the canals.

HOW DO CANALS CLIMB HILLS?

WATER, left to its own devices, always flows from its highest point to its lowest, until the two points are on the same level. If a canal sloped as it climbed a hill, its water would simply flow to the bottom. One solution is to bore a tunnel through the hill, so that the canal can continue on a level course, but sometimes this is too costly or geologically impossible. Building locks can solve this problem.

A lock consists of two gates across the canal, with mechanisms for opening them on the towpath.

To climb to a higher level of the canal, a boat enters the first lock gate, which is closed behind it.

Paddles in the second lock gate are opened so that water can flow in, gradually raising the level of water in the lock.

When the water ahead is level with that in the lock, the gates are opened and the boat can move on.

ARE ROAD SIGNS INTERNATIONAL?

ALTHOUGH ROAD SIGNS do differ across the world, many rely on pictures and symbols rather than words. These are often faster for the motorist to recognize, and avoid some language problems for international travellers.

Whatever language a traveller understands, this sign is very clear.

HOW IS PAPER MADE?

Paper is made from plant fibres. These are very tiny cellulose tubes that make up the stem or leaves of a plant. The fibres are mixed with water and then poured onto a mesh, so that the water can drain through, leaving the fibres behind. The mat of fibres is rolled and dried until it becomes a strong sheet of paper. Although traditionally paper was made by hand, today it is usually made in one large machine, which takes in the water and fibres at one end and produces reels of paper at the other end.

HOW ARE DIFFERENT PAPERS DESCRIBED?

THERE is no such thing as good or bad paper, just paper that is good or bad for a particular job. Blotting paper needs to be able to absorb ink, for example, while paper for printing must let the ink sit on the surface, so that the printing is crisp and clear. Most paper is described firstly by weight. Paper for a children's picture book might weigh 150 grams per square metre. It is said to be 150gsm paper.

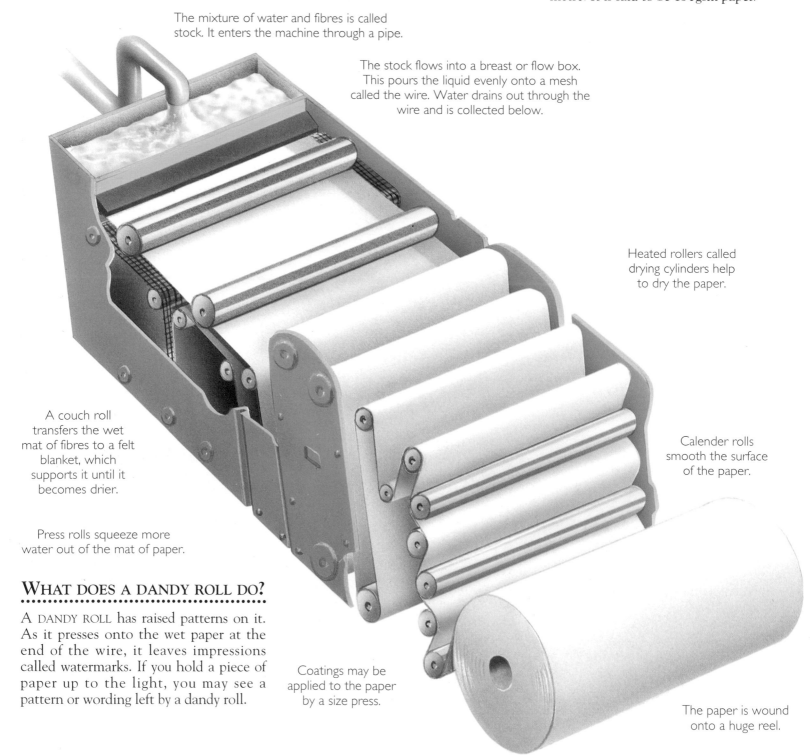

The mixture of water and fibres is called stock. It enters the machine through a pipe.

The stock flows into a breast or flow box. This pours the liquid evenly onto a mesh called the wire. Water drains out through the wire and is collected below.

Heated rollers called drying cylinders help to dry the paper.

A couch roll transfers the wet mat of fibres to a felt blanket, which supports it until it becomes drier.

Calender rolls smooth the surface of the paper.

Press rolls squeeze more water out of the mat of paper.

WHAT DOES A DANDY ROLL DO?

A DANDY ROLL has raised patterns on it. As it presses onto the wet paper at the end of the wire, it leaves impressions called watermarks. If you hold a piece of paper up to the light, you may see a pattern or wording left by a dandy roll.

Coatings may be applied to the paper by a size press.

The paper is wound onto a huge reel.

fast facts

HOW CAN YOU MEASURE A PAPER'S OPACITY?

Nowadays a computer can test how opaque paper is (how difficult it is to see through it). A simpler test is to draw a letter in thick black ink on a piece of paper and then place sheets of the paper to be tested on top of it until the letter can no longer be seen. The fewer sheets needed, the more opaque the paper.

HOW IS PAPER RECYCLED?

It is easy to recycle paper. Old paper is soaked in water and put into a giant liquidizer, to blend it into stock. This is poured into the paper-making machine in the usual way.

WHAT IS PAPIER MÂCHÉ?

Papier mâché is French for "torn paper." Paper is torn or cut into small pieces. These are then pasted in layers over a mould. When the glue and the paper are dry, the mould can be removed and the article decorated. Bowls, boxes and even furniture can be made like this.

WHAT IS THE GRAIN OF A PIECE OF PAPER?

If you try to tear an article out of a newspaper, you will find that it tears in quite a straight line in one direction but not in the other. That is because the movement of the wire causes the fibres to settle in one direction, giving the paper a grain. When paper is printed, it is important that the direction of the grain is known, or the pages will buckle.

WHO INVENTED THE FIRST PAPERMAKING MACHINE?

Louis Robert, a Frenchman, invented a papermaking machine in 1799. Four years later, the Fourdrinier brothers in London developed the idea. Papermaking machines are still called Fourdrinier machines today.

WHAT KIND OF PLANT FIBRE IS USED TO MAKE PAPER?

NOWADAYS most paper is made from specially grown trees. These trees are usually softwoods, grown in the cooler parts of the world where little else can thrive. Fir, pine, spruce, larch and cedar trees are all used. The trees do not have to be very tall or straight, as they do for timber. Almost all parts of the tree, except the bark, can be ground up into fibres for papermaking.

Felled trees are heavy. Where possible, the trunks are floated down a river to the sawmill, where they are ground up into fibres.

HOW IS STRONG CARDBOARD MADE?

CARDBOARD is really just very thick paper. The machine that makes it is slightly different because the card is not wound onto a reel at the end, but cut up into sheets. For making strong, light boxes, corrugated cardboard is often used. This has paper pressed into a ridged shape sandwiched between two outer sheets.

WHERE WAS PAPER FIRST MADE?

PAPER WAS FIRST MADE 2000 years ago in China. It was made from pulped rags and old fishing nets, drained on a sieve made of bamboo! Paper may not immediately seem to be an ideal building material, but it is light and cheap, and allows a certain amount of light to pass through it. It is ideal for use with bamboo, which is also very light. Paper has been used in China and Japan for centuries to make screens and internal sliding walls in houses. Although these are not soundproof, they are very attractive and easily replaced if damaged.

CAN PAPER ONLY BE MADE FROM WOOD FIBRES?

PAPER can be made from almost any kind of plant fibre. In some parts of the world, banana stalks and sugar-cane stems made fine, strong paper. On the whole, the longer the fibres, the stronger the paper.

Paper money is folded, pushed into wallets and pockets, and passed from hand to hand. It needs to be very strong. A special paper is made that may contain cotton fibres (which come from cotton plants) or linen fibres (from flax plants).

WHEN WAS PRINTING INVENTED?

Printing – producing identical copies of a picture or piece of writing by pressing an inked block onto a surface – was introduced by the Chinese over a thousand years ago. However, the breakthrough of movable type, which meant that a new block could be made up from existing pieces of type, without having to carve it from scratch, was developed in 1438 by Johannes Gutenberg, in Germany. This was still a fairly slow, manual method, although much faster than the alternative of writing documents out by hand. It was not until the invention of steam and, later, electrical machinery to power the presses that documents could be printed rapidly on a large scale.

HOW MANY COLOURS ARE USED IN COLOUR PRINTING?

HOWEVER COLOURFUL a page in a book may be, it is probably made up of only four colours. Tiny dots of yellow, blue, red and black inks are used to print the page. The dots are so small that they cannot usually be seen with the naked eye. Instead, they "mix" visually to form all the colours on the final page.

WHAT IS REGISTRATION?

THE PAGE to be printed passes between inked rollers or plates four times, each time with a different coloured ink being used. In order to make sure that the final image is clear and sharp, the four printings must line up exactly on top of each other. This is known as registration. Registration marks, at the corners of a page, help the printer to position the images accurately. You may have seen a strip of coloured shapes on the edge of a printed food packet. These also enable the printer to see at a glance if the four printings have been properly positioned.

Registration marks normally fall outside the main printed area. When the pages are trimmed to their final size, the marks are cut off.

A photograph is scanned to separate the image into a piece of film for each of the four "process" colours.

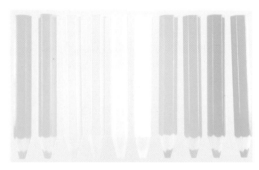

The shade of blue used in four-colour printing is called cyan.

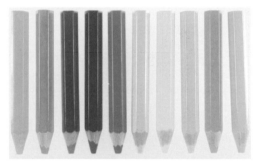

The red ink is a pinkish colour called magenta. Brighter reds are created when magenta is added to yellow.

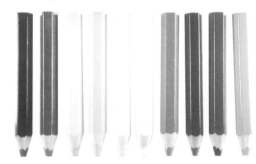

Black ink gives a deeper black than mixing the three other colours and gives crisper black type.

When the four colour separations are printed one on top of the other, a full-colour picture is produced.

HOW ARE DIFFERENT TONES OF COLOUR PRINTED?

SOME PRINTED IMAGES use one solid colour. These words are printed in solid black ink, for example. The dots are so close together that no background colour shows through. Using increasingly widely spaced dots creates the impression of paler tones of grey.

| 100%
cyan | 50%
cyan | 30%
cyan | 10%
cyan |

The tone of a colour being printed is described by the percentage of paper that is covered with ink.

WHAT IS A TYPEFACE?

A TYPEFACE is an alphabet that has been specially designed for printing. It can usually be used in a variety of sizes and styles. The typeface chosen has a huge effect on how a printed page looks. Some typefaces are designed to be easy to read. Others are meant to catch the eye in headings and titles. Today, computers make it easy to manipulate type, **stretching it** or squashing it, for example, to create special effects. It is also easy to adapt typefaces or create your own. Each set of letters, numbers and symbols in a typeface is called a font.

WHY CAN THE NUMBER OF PAGES IN A BOOK USUALLY BE DIVIDED EXACTLY BY 16?

PAGES IN A BOOK are not printed one by one. They are printed on huge sheets of paper that then pass through another machine to be folded. When the book is bound (put into its cover), the edges of the pages are cut on a guillotine. A piece of paper folded in half creates four pages. Larger sheets of paper are folded to make 16, 32 or even 64 pages.

HOW IS A HARDBACK BOOK COVER MADE?

GLUEING, sewing or stapling pages together and placing them within a cover is called binding. Several pieces of card and paper are required to bind a hardback book. It is also possible to add bookmark ribbons and little pieces of fabric called headbands at the top and bottom of the spine (back) of the book.

Pieces of card are glued to a printed cover paper, the edges of which are folded over.

The book block is placed in the cover (or case).

Endpapers – the first and last pages of the book block or separate pieces of paper – are glued down to hold the book block in place.

fast facts

WHY ARE THE EVEN-NUMBERED PAGES OF A BOOK ALWAYS ON THE LEFT?

Any leaf of a book has two sides (two pages). The first lefthand page of a book is the second side of the first righthand page. If that is page 1, then its other side must be page 2, and every other lefthand page in the book will have an even number.

WHAT DO RECTO AND VERSO MEAN?

A recto page is the righthand page of a book, wherever it is opened. If that page is turned, its other side is known as the verso. So this is a recto page, and page 152 is its verso.

WHAT IS A SERIF?

Some typefaces, such as this one, have little strokes, called serifs, at the ends of some letters. The typeface used in this book for labels to pictures has no strokes and is called a sans serif (without serifs) typeface.

WHAT ARE PROOFS?

Before thousands of copies of a book or magazine are printed, the publisher needs to be sure that everything is right. A few copies of the pages, called proofs, are printed on a special press so that they can be checked before a larger press gets to work on the bulk of the copies.

WHAT IS A CO-EDITION?

Printing presses are massive machines. It takes a long time to get them ready to print, and that time has to be paid for. The more copies that are printed, the cheaper each one is, as the cost of making ready the machine is divided between them. By changing the black plate halfway through a job, a version of the pages in another language can be printed, without the cost of making the presses ready again. This is called a co-edition.

WHAT IS A TEXTILE?

The word "textile" may be used to describe any woven material, or, more broadly, any cloth. Most fabrics are made from threads. These may be looped or passed under and over each other to create a firm cloth, or they may simply be matted together to form a kind of felt. There are thousands of different kinds of textile, each with its own properties and uses.

WHERE DO FIBRES FOR TEXTILES COME FROM?

AT ONE TIME, fibres for textiles came from either plants or animals. The former included cotton from the cotton plant and linen from flax, but also coarser fibres for rope, sacking and matting, such as hemp, jute, sisal and even coconut fibres. Animal-based fibres have been spun from the coats of sheep, goats, camels, llamas and, by real enthusiasts, dogs! Nowadays, there are also artificial fibres, spun from mixtures of chemicals. By mixing different fibres together, it is possible to make fabrics for every purpose.

Spun threads are twisted together for strength, forming yarn of different thicknesses.

WHAT IS SPINNING?

THREADS from plants and animals are usually not more than a few centimetres long. To make a long, strong thread for weaving or knitting, they must be spun. A carding machine combs the fibres so that they are all lying in the same direction and form a loose rope. This rope is then gently drawn out into a thinner thread and twisted into yarn.

These loose ropes of cotton fibres are called slivers. They will gradually be pulled into a thinner rope, called roving, before being twisted into thread. Years ago, this process was done by hand, using a spinning wheel.

Dyed thread may be wound onto small reels for sewing at home, or huge reels for use on powerful industrial weaving, knitting or sewing machines.

HOW ARE THREADS AND TEXTILES COLOURED?

SUBSTANCES called dyes are used to colour threads and textiles. In the past, natural dyes were used, made mainly from plants. Onion skins, for example, give a soft, reddish colour. Most natural dyes fade gradually when washed or exposed to light, which can be very attractive. Many people like the faded colour of denim jeans, for example, dyed with a natural plant-based dye called indigo. Modern chemical dyes do not fade so easily. They give strong, bright colours. Either skeins of thread or finished fabrics may be dyed by passing them through a dye bath, then fixing the dye with other chemicals and drying the result.

WHAT IS THE DIFFERENCE BETWEEN KNITTING AND WEAVING?

BOTH KNITTING AND WEAVING are methods of making threads into cloth, but knitting involves looping one long thread together, while weaving usually involves passing threads lying in one direction over and under threads lying at right angles to them.

In handweaving, the loom holds the lengthways threads (warp), while the weaver passes a shuttle, carrying the crossways thread (weft) between them. The finished fabric cannot be wider than the weaver's outstretched arms.

Threads in woven fabrics can be crisscrossed in hundreds of different ways to add texture to the cloth.

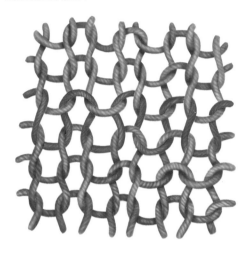

It is not only woollen jumpers that are knitted. The fabric that T-shirts are made from is knitted cotton.

HOW ARE FABRICS PATTERNED?

THERE ARE TWO main ways of patterning fabrics. By using coloured threads in the knitting or weaving, patterns can be made in the fabric itself. This is a very easy way to create stripes and checks, and it is quite cheap to use lots of colours, so the resulting fabric can be very bright. Another method of patterning fabric is to print it, using special dyes. This may be done by big rollers or by squeezing dye through patterned screens. Since only one colour can be printed at a time, each additional colour adds to the cost.

When threads of different colours pass under and over each other, it is as if the colours mix. Here black and cream threads combine to make a grey colour.

WHAT IS SILK MADE FROM?

NATURAL SILK is spun as a thread by silkworms. They use it to form a cocoon. Unlike other natural threads, the silkworm's thread is very long – up to one kilometre (0.62 miles). Traditionally made in Asia, silk was such a sought-after textile that the route from Europe to the East became known as the Great Silk Road.

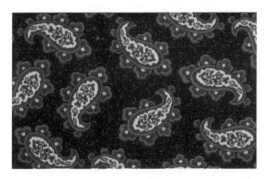

The curved shapes on this printed fabric are described as paisley, after a town in Scotland, although this was originally an Indian design.

HOW LONG DOES IT TAKE TO SHEAR A SHEEP?

IN 1957, a New Zealander sheared a sheep in just 47 seconds!

Expert shearers can remove the fleece from hundreds of sheep in a day.

WHO WAS THE FIRST PHOTOGRAPHER?

The first person to take a photograph was a Frenchman, Joseph Nicéphore Niepce, in 1822. However, as is often the case with new inventions, many other scientists had been experimenting with light, lenses and light-sensitive chemicals. Working with Niepce was a man called Louis Daguerre, who later improved on Niepce's process. Some early photographs were called daguerreotypes.

HOW DOES A CAMERA WORK?

A CAMERA is a lightproof box containing light-sensitive film. To take a picture, the photographer presses a button to open a shutter and let light pass through the aperture, a hole in the front of the camera. The camera's lens focuses the light so that it forms a sharp image on the photographic film, just as the lenses in our eyes focus the light onto our retinas. Then the shutter closes again so that no more light reaches the film. The whole process usually takes just a fraction of a second.

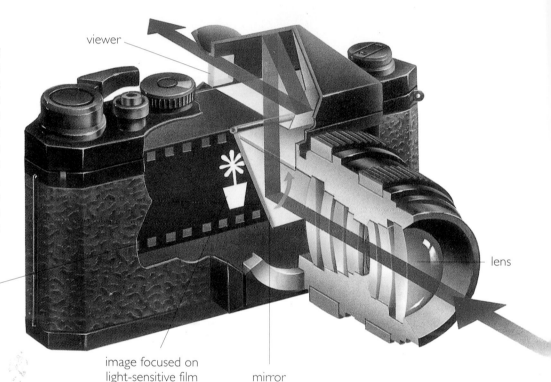

viewer

lens

sprocket holes guide the film through the camera

image focused on light-sensitive film

mirror

When the camera is not in use, a lens cap stops dirt and grit from getting onto the lens.

HOW IS FILM DEVELOPED?

AFTER AN IMAGE has been recorded on light-sensitive film in a camera, the film is moved along, so that the next photograph will be taken on a fresh piece of film. No more light must hit the exposed film until it is developed, or the picture would be spoiled. When all the photographs on a roll of film have been taken, the film is wound into its case, which is lightproof. The development process then takes place in a darkroom, or in a specially made machine.

The film is taken out of its case and immersed in a chemical solution that develops the image.

After rinsing, the film is bathed in more chemicals to fix the image onto the film.

A final rinse and the film is dried. The image is negative: dark areas look light and vice versa.

HOW ARE FILMS PRINTED?

PRINTING converts the negative image of the film into a positive image on paper. Light is shone through the film onto light-sensitive paper. Passing the light through lenses makes the image larger. The print is then developed and fixed just as the film was.

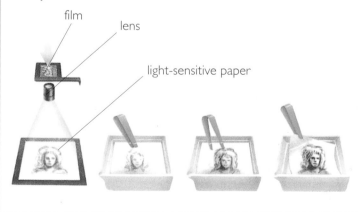

film

lens

light-sensitive paper

HOW CAN PHOTOGRAPHS BE MADE TO MOVE?

MOVING PICTURES, or movies, do not really have moving images at all. They are simply a series of still photographs, shown rapidly one after the other. Our brains are not able to distinguish the individual images at that speed, so we see what appears to be a moving picture.

HOW CAN LENSES CHANGE OUR VIEW?

THE WAY in which we see the world has been greatly influenced by photography. We are used to seeing printed images that we could never see with our naked eyes, either because they happen too fast, or because a special camera lens has allowed an extraordinary view to be taken.

Macrophotography is a way of photographing very small objects by using special macro lenses. Used for both still and moving pictures, macrophotography has transformed our knowledge of the way that tiny living things, such as insects, behave.

These Chicago skyscrapers do not really lean so alarmingly, but by using a special lens, the photographer has been able to emphasize the way in which the massive buildings tower over the church in the foreground of the picture.

Once only wealthy people could have pictures of themselves, painted by an artist. Now most people have family photographs. Before photography, we could only see mirror images of ourselves in a looking glass. Now we can see ourselves as others see us.

fast facts

WHERE DOES THE WORD "CINEMA" COME FROM?

"Cinema" (or "kinema" as it was originally) comes from a Greek word meaning "movement".

WHY DO CARRIAGE WHEELS APPEAR TO GO BACKWARDS IN MOVIES?

As the carriage moves forward, the spokes of its wheels go round, but a movie is just a series of still pictures. Because we cannot distinguish between the different spokes, it can appear that the same spoke is seen in a slightly earlier position each time, when in fact it is simply another spoke that has moved forward that is being seen.

HOW DOES COLOUR FILM WORK?

Colour film has three layers, each sensitive to blue, green or red light. When colour film is processed, the layers are coloured with yellow, magenta and cyan dyes to produce the full-colour image.

WHAT IS A POLAROID CAMERA?

A Polaroid camera uses special film that can develop itself. When the picture has been taken, chemicals are released onto the film, and the final image appears within a minute.

WHICH WAS THE FIRST MOVIE TO HAVE ITS OWN SOUND TRACK?

Full-length movies were silent until 1927, when *The Jazz Singer* was released by Warner Brothers.

WHERE IS BOLLYWOOD?

Just as the movie industry of the United States is based in Hollywood, California, the thriving movie industry of India is centred on Bombay, nicknamed "Bollywood".

WHEN WERE RADIO WAVES FIRST USED TO SEND A MESSAGE?

Although several scientists, including Heinrich Hertz, experimented with sending and receiving radio waves, the first person to patent a useful system for using them to send signals through the air was an Italian engineer called Gugliemo Marconi (1874–1937) in 1896. He created enormous publicity for his work by claiming to have sent the first radio signal across the Atlantic in 1901. Today there is disagreement about whether such a signal was received, but Marconi was right that sending radio messages between Europe and the Americas was possible, and his work encouraged the enthusiasm for and development of radio communications that continues to this day. As Marconi's messages did not pass through wires, the system was known as wireless telegraphy.

A	• – –	S	• • •
B	– • • •	T	–
C	– • – •	U	• • –
D	– • •	V	• • • –
E	•	W	• – –
F	• • – •	X	– • • –
G	– – •	Y	– • – –
H	• • • •	Z	– – • •
I	• •		
J	• – – –	1	• – – – –
K	– • –	2	• • – – –
L	• – • •	3	• • • – –
M	– –	4	• • • • –
N	– •	5	• • • • •
O	– – –	6	– • • • •
P	• – – •	7	– – • • •
Q	– – • –	8	– – – • •
R	• – •	9	– – – – •

WHY WAS MORSE CODE INVENTED?

MORSE CODE was ideal for sending messages by telegraph because it used only two kinds of signal: a long one, called a dash, and a short one, called a dot. By sending long and short bursts of radio waves along a wire, a transmitter could send a clear message. Samuel Morse (1791–1872) was an American engineer who invented a practical magnetic telegraph. His invention was more or less ignored on both sides of the Atlantic, until, in 1843, the United States government allotted 30,000 dollars for a telegraph line between Washington and Baltimore. Morse invented Morse Code for use on his telegraph, which became very successful.

WHY HAVE RADIO MESSAGES BEEN BEAMED INTO SPACE?

NO ONE KNOWS if we are alone in the universe. In order to try to make contact with other intelligent life forms in our galaxy, some laboratories regularly send radio signals out into space. In fact, distant constellations do emit radio waves, but so far they do not seem to have been transmitted intentionally by living creatures. Scientists watch for a regular pattern of signals that might indicate a living transmitter.

WHAT ARE TELECOMMUNICATIONS?

TELECOMMUNICATIONS include sending and receiving messages by radio, television, telephone and fax. They began when the telegraph used electrical pulses, sent down a wire, to send information. Radio waves, electricity, or light can carry telecommunications. As well as a method of carrying the message, telecommunications also require a transmitter, to send the signals, and a receiver.

Modern telecommunications make it possible for people all over the world to make contact with each other, however remote their locations.

HOW DOES A TELEVISION SHOW PICTURES?

TELEVISION TECHNOLOGY uses electric signals through cables or ultra-high frequency (UHF) radio waves to transmit pictures and sound to a television set, which acts as a receiver. The signals come into the television through a cable or an aerial. The picture signals are divided into three – one each for red, green and blue. In the television, there is an electron gun for each colour, which fires electron beams (also known as cathode rays) onto the screen. The screen is covered with chemicals called phosphors. The electron beams scan rapidly across the screen, causing tiny dots of phosphors to glow red, green and blue. Viewed with normal vision, from a distance, the dots blur into a full-colour picture.

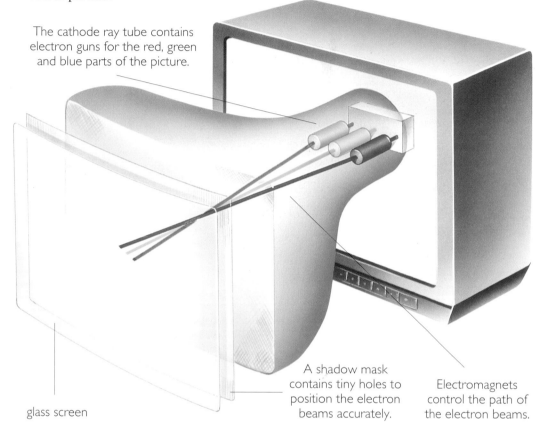

The cathode ray tube contains electron guns for the red, green and blue parts of the picture.

glass screen

A shadow mask contains tiny holes to position the electron beams accurately.

Electromagnets control the path of the electron beams.

HOW CAN RADIOS HELP NATURALISTS?

BY PUTTING COLLARS with radio transmitters onto wild animals, naturalists have been able to track their movements, night and day, adding enormously to our knowledge of animal behaviour. The collars do not interfere with the animals' normal lives. As well as learning about animal migrations and hunting patterns, naturalists are also able to discover more about the life span of animals in the wild, which may differ enormously from that of those kept in zoos and wildlife parks.

Polar bears can be fiercely protective of their young, and the conditions of the Arctic in winter make it difficult for naturalists to follow their movements. A harmless tranquillizer is used to send the animal to sleep while a transmitting collar is fitted.

HOW DOES A VIDEO RECORDER WORK?

A VIDEO RECORDER stores television sound and pictures on a magnetic tape. It receives the electric signal that comes through a cable or aerial into the machine, then records it on tape in much the same way as a tape recorder does, although the video recorder makes diagonal tracks so that more information can be held on the tape. A record–replay head in the video recorder enables the information on tape to be sent to a television set.

CAN SENDERS OF MORSE CODE BE ANONYMOUS?

Of course, the receiver of a message in Morse Code may be thousands of miles away from its sender, so he or she may not be sure who is pressing the Morse key. But when sending Morse manually, everyone has his or her own style and rhythm. An experienced Morse receiver can often recognize the sender by the way the message is sent, just as we may recognize the sender of a letter by his or her handwriting.

HOW DO RADIO WAVES ACT AS BABYSITTERS?

Many parents with small children use baby alarms. These transmit radio signals of the sounds a child makes to a receiving radio in another room or even a nearby home. They can help to reassure a parent that a child is still sleeping while they are out of hearing range.

WHAT IS CLOSED-CIRCUIT TELEVISION?

Closed-circuit television, which is most commonly used for security purposes, is a system in which the television pictures travel directly from the camera taking them to a screen. This does not mean that they cannot be stored. The pictures can be captured on videotape in the normal way.

Videotape has many uses in sport. For example, it may be used for an "action replay", to check what really happened in a fast-moving sport. Athletes are also able to study videotape in order to see where they are making errors and so improve their technique.

WHAT WAS THE EARLIEST SOUND RECORDING?

In 1877, the American inventor Thomas Edison (1847–1931) experimented with a machine called a "phonograph", which converted sound vibrations into grooves on a cylinder covered with tinfoil. A sharp needle, called a stylus, was attached to a diaphragm at the narrow end of a large horn. When sound waves travelled into the horn, they made the diaphragm vibrate, causing the needle to move up and down, and cutting a groove of varying depth in the tinfoil. If this process was reversed, so that the needle was made to run over the grooves, it caused the diaphragm to vibrate. Vibrations passed through the horn, pushing air in front of them, to reach the listener's ear as sound. Later, wax-coated cylinders were used instead of tinfoil, to give a better result.

HOW DOES A CASSETTE TAPE RECORD AND PLAY?

DISCS were the main method of recording and playing music for the first half of the twentieth century, but sound recording on steel tape was used in the 1930s by radio stations. In 1935, two German companies developed a strong plastic tape, which had a layer of iron oxide on the surface. This invention eventually made it possible for smaller, domestic tape recorders to come into use. In 1963, Philips introduced something they called a "compact cassette", which contained a thin tape within a plastic case. This was much lighter and more convenient for home use.

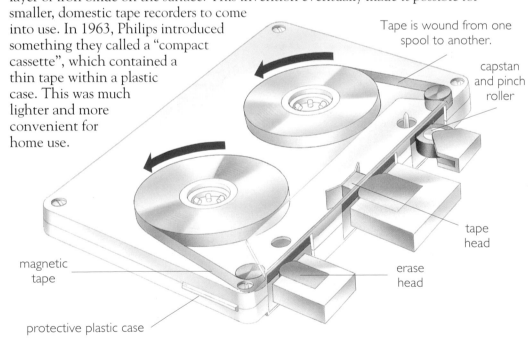

Tape is wound from one spool to another.

capstan and pinch roller

tape head

magnetic tape

erase head

protective plastic case

On blank magnetic tape, the magnetized particles are all facing in the same direction. Electrical signals created by recorded sounds cause the magnetized particles to move into patterns that match the sound signal. When the tape is played, the head "reads" the magnetized particles and creates electrical signals to match them, which are relayed to a loudspeaker to be played. In order to wipe the recording from the tape, all that needs to happen is for the tape to be passed through a strong magnetic field, which lines up the magnetized particles once more.

WHO INVENTED THE GRAMOPHONE?

In 1888, the German-American inventor Emile Berliner (1851–1929) invented a system of sound recording that could be mass produced. He devised a flat disc, called a gramophone record. On the disc, a groove ran in a spiral from the outer edge of the disc to the centre. Side-to-side, rather than up-and-down movements of the stylus recorded and played the sound vibrations. Once one disc had been made, it could be used as a mould to make a metal die, which could then stamp out exact copies of the disc in large numbers.

In the second half of the twentieth century, magnetic tape has been an important storage medium for sound and computerized information. Today compact discs and other recording methods are taking over.

HOW DOES A COMPACT DISC WORK?

A COMPACT DISC (CD) has a plastic surface on which sounds are stored in binary code as very small holes, called pits, and flat areas, called lands. These can be "read" by a laser beam. The laser beam scans across the surface of the disc. When the light falls on a pit, it is scattered, but when it falls on a land, it is reflected back to a light-sensitive detector. This in turn causes a pulse of current to pass to a loudspeaker, which converts it back into sound.

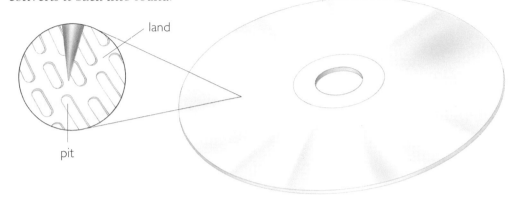

land

pit

As the laser scans the disc, a motor spins the CD round. CDs can be used to store words and pictures as well as sounds. The photographs in this book were stored on compact discs before being used.

HOW DO MICROPHONES WORK?

INSIDE A MICROPHONE is a metal disc, called a diaphragm. When a sound wave hits the sensitive diaphragm, it makes it vibrate at the same frequency. This causes a wire coil, beneath the diaphragm, to move up and down. As the coil comes near to a magnet below, it creates a pulse of electric current in the wire. The pattern of these pulses matches the pattern of the sound wave. The pulses can be sent along a wire to a loudspeaker, to be turned back into sound, or they can be recorded on a tape or compact disc.

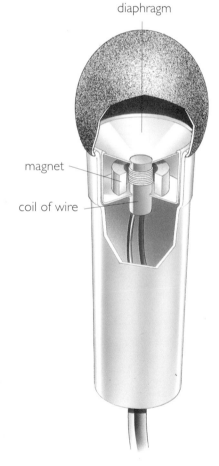

diaphragm

magnet

coil of wire

Microphones and loudspeakers make it possible for huge numbers of people to hear speakers or performers at public events. For actors and singers, very small microphones can now be attached to their faces, near their cheekbones, so that the audience cannot see them at all.

fast facts

WHY DID SINGERS ONCE PERFORM IN CAVES?

We do not hear our own voices as others hear them, because the sounds pass through flesh and bone to reach our ears. Today singers can hear recordings of their voices, but before sound recording, the only way they could judge their own singing was to perform in a cave and listen to the echo!

HOW CAN RECORDINGS HELP HISTORIANS?

Written records give historians lots of useful information, but do not tell the whole story. Recordings of the voices of ordinary people, recalling their own views and memories, give vivid pictures of the past. Imagine how interesting it would be to hear people from five hundred years ago speaking. In four hundred years time, that will be possible!

WHAT IS SAMPLING?

Sampling involves recording different sounds and then using digital technology to manipulate them, changing pitch, volume, tone and tempo to create special effects.

Face microphones are very useful in musical theatre, where actors have to sing and dance at the same time.

HOW DOES A LOUDSPEAKER PRODUCE SOUND?

A LOUDSPEAKER works like a reversed microphone. Electric current flows into a coil of wire, turning it into an electromagnet. This attracts the coil to another magnet inside the loudspeaker, causing the coil to vibrate. This vibrates a diaphragm at the same frequency as the original sound, pushing air in front of it to carry the sound to the ears of the listeners. Many loudspeakers can be connected together, so that sound is heard all around a large outdoor or indoor space.

DID EARLY BUILDERS HAVE PLANS TO FOLLOW?

For thousands of years, people have been building homes, temples and monuments, but until only a few centuries ago, they had no proper plans to follow before building began. They based their work on tried and tested methods, estimating how strongly walls had to be built to support the floors above and the roof. Of course, many buildings collapsed or subsided, but others are still standing to this day, a tribute to the skill of builders in times past.

HOW WERE THE PYRAMIDS BUILT?

THE EGYPTIANS were building massive pyramids almost 5000 years ago. We are still not sure how they achieved this without the mechanical lifting and cutting equipment that we have today, but the answer must be that they used huge numbers of slaves to shape and haul the enormous stones with which they built. Recently, scientists have calculated that as many as 10,000 slaves were probably needed to work on these structures.

WHAT ARE THE EARLIEST BUILDINGS KNOWN?

THE EARLIEST HUMAN HOMES that we know of are caves. We know that they were inhabited because paintings have been found on the walls, but these homes were not built – they were made by nature, not human beings. The earliest mud and wooden shelters and huts have not survived intact, but from about 2700BC people began to build some of the huge stone structures that have survived to this day. Apart from the Egyptian pyramids, one of the earliest was the circle of stones known as Stonehenge, in England. It is not known exactly what this was for, but it probably had religious significance. Throughout history, religion has spurred builders to create many of the largest and most impressive buildings ever seen.

DO ALL HUMAN SOCIETIES BUILD HOMES?

WHEN PREHISTORIC PEOPLES began to farm, they built settlements. However, some peoples preferred to continue to move about in search of food, following a nomadic lifestyle. Nomads do not need settled homes, but they do need shelter from the weather, so many of them carry tents made of skins or woven fabric. Tents are light to carry and can be put up very quickly.

Some Native Americans made shelters from skins and sticks. A hole in the top let out smoke.

HOW HAVE BUILDING STYLES DEVELOPED THROUGH HISTORY?

ALTHOUGH many traditional building styles are still in use, the appearance of buildings and the way in which they are built changes as outside influences are brought to bear on their architects and builders. Naturally, buildings are based on shapes that give the strongest structures: rectangles, cylinders, triangles and domes. In the search for new forms, architects have often looked back to the past. In the fourteenth century in Italy, for example, designers rediscovered the architecture of ancient Rome and neo-classical ("new" classical) buildings in the subsequent centuries were built all over the world, especially where a building was meant to embody power, learning and dignity. New buildings today still combine recent ideas with traditional motifs.

| Doric column | Ionic column | Corinthian column |

Classical styles of architecture were divided into orders, of which the Doric, Ionic and Corinthian were three that may still frequently be seen on large houses, churches and public buildings.

fast facts

WHICH ARE THE BEST BUILDING MATERIALS?

On the whole, building materials are not better than one another. Some are simply more suitable in some situations and for some purposes than others. Traditionally, people have built with the materials nearest to hand, using wood in forest areas, mud in dry areas, and bricks where there was clay to make them. The towering structures built today require modern building materials, such as reinforced steel, concrete and glass.

HOW IS CONCRETE REINFORCED?

Used since the 1850s, reinforced concrete has metal bars or wires embedded in it for extra strength.

WHAT WAS A ZIGGURAT?

Ruins of ziggurats can still be seen. They were ancient Mesopotamian stepped towers, with temples on top.

WHAT DO AN ARCHITECT'S PLANS SHOW?

AN ARCHITECT'S plans give all the information needed to build the structure shown. The plans show the materials to be used, how they fit together, and all the measurements necessary to complete the building. Plans usually show several elevations (different views) of the structure, including a floor plan and a plan of each side of the building. Nowadays, computers are increasingly used to draw up plans. They can provide lists of the materials and equipment needed as the plans are drawn, and work out costings.

IS CONCRETE A NEW BUILDING MATERIAL?

CONCRETE is a mixture of sand, water and cement, a powder made of lime and clay. Far from being a new material, concrete was used by the Romans in the first century AD to build the dome of the Pantheon in Rome.

HOW ARE SKYSCRAPERS BUILT?

SKYSCRAPERS have a frame, usually made of steel or concrete, to support the floors and walls, which are attached to the frame. The frame is rather like the skeleton inside a human body. It is not designed to be completely rigid, but to sway a little in high winds, thus reducing the force of the wind upon the structure.

WHAT ARE CERAMICS?

Ceramics are objects made of materials that are permanently hardened by being heated. Usually, the word is used to mean articles made of various forms of clay. Sticky clay is dug from the Earth and needs to have impurities, such as stones, removed before it can be used. The clay may be naturally red, yellow, grey or almost white, but can be coloured before shaping or covered with a coloured glaze.

WHAT CAN BE MADE FROM CLAY?

CLAY CAN BE USED to make a huge variety of ceramic articles, from tiny electronic components to bricks and baths. It is a good insulator and, when covered with a glaze, is completely waterproof. Unlike many metals, glazed clay is unreactive, so that acidic foods will not stain it, and exposure to water and the air will not tarnish or corrode it.

HOW ARE CLAY ARTICLES SHAPED?

CLAY CAN BE SHAPED when it is wet by squeezing it between the fingers, "throwing" it on a potter's wheel, or pushing it into a mould. Before using any of these methods, the potter must make sure that there are no air bubbles in the clay. If there are, the air will expand when the clay is baked, and the article may explode, breaking other items in the kiln as well. However ceramic articles are produced, they are made a little larger than the finished product needs to be, as they shrink slightly when baked.

A potter's wheel consists of a turntable, powered by a treadle or motor. The clay is placed (or "thrown") into the middle of the wheel and shaped with wet hands or tools as it turns. A skilled potter can make a perfectly symmetrical pot in this way.

Mass-produced items are usually produced by moulding. A machine called a jolley pushes a piece of clay into a mug-shaped mould. Then a profiling tool presses round inside to push the clay against the sides of the mould and leave the inside of the mug empty. The handle is added later.

WHY ARE CERAMICS BAKED?

CERAMICS are baked to make them hard and waterproof. Until they are baked (fired), ceramics can be mixed with water again to form clay. Firing is done in a large oven called a kiln. In large ceramics factories, the kilns are heated all the time. They are like long tunnels, through which ceramics move slowly on trolleys in a never-ending process. The first firing that a clay article receives is called a biscuit firing. It makes the article hard and brittle, but it is still porous. Water can be absorbed by it.

Pots for plants grown outside need to be chosen carefully if the gardener lives in an area that has frosts in the winter. If the pots are too porous, they will absorb a lot of water. If this freezes, it will expand and crack the pot.

This Chinese bowl has intricate patterns painted onto it in coloured glazes. In English, some kinds of pottery are often called "china". This is because fine pottery was first imported from China.

Glazes often change colour in the kiln, so test pieces of clay, dipped in glaze, are fired to make sure that the colour will come out as required.

HOW IS POTTERY DECORATED?

THERE ARE MANY WAYS of decorating pots. They can be dipped in a glaze, made of tiny particles of glass in a liquid, and fired for a second time. The glassy covering melts onto the pottery, making it completely waterproof. Pottery can also be decorated after glazing, with transfers, hand-painted designs, or by screen-printing. It may then be fired for a third time to fix the decoration.

WHAT IS SLIP?

SLIP IS A MIXTURE of clay and water, forming a thick liquid. It can be used as a kind of glue to stick a handle onto a cup when both are "leather hard" (hard enough to handle but still soft enough to cut with a knife). Slip can also be poured into plaster moulds to form intricate shapes. The plaster absorbs water from the slip, causing it to dry on the outside first. If the rest of the slip is poured away, hollow vessels and ornaments can be made.

WHY ARE THERE UNGLAZED PARTS ON THE UNDERSIDE OF A CERAMIC OBJECT?

IN THE HEAT of the kiln, glaze would fuse with the shelf that the object stands on, so glaze is carefully wiped from the base of the object before it is fired.

WHAT IS GLASS MADE OF?

Glass is an extraordinarily useful material. The substances from which it is made are easy to find and very cheap. Glass is mainly melted, cooled sand, but other ingredients are added, such as sodium carbonate (soda ash) and limestone. Although it appears solid to us, glass is in fact a liquid, flowing incredibly slowly. When windows that are hundreds of years old are measured, they are found to be slightly thicker at the bottom than at the top, as the glass very gradually flows downwards.

Coloured glass is made by adding metallic oxides, such as iron, copper, manganese and chromium.

HOW IS PLATE GLASS MADE?

PLATE GLASS is thick, good quality glass made in huge sheets for shop windows. Its very smooth surface is made by floating the molten glass onto a bath of molten tin. Tin melts at a lower temperature than glass, so the glass begins to set on the tin and is then passed over rollers as it finishes cooling. The larger the bath of molten tin, the larger the glass that can be made.

HOW IS GLASS CUT?

HARDENED METAL BLADES can cut glass but are easily blunted. More often, glass is cut with the hardest natural substance known – a diamond. If a furrow is made in glass with a diamond, it will usually break cleanly when pressure is applied to it.

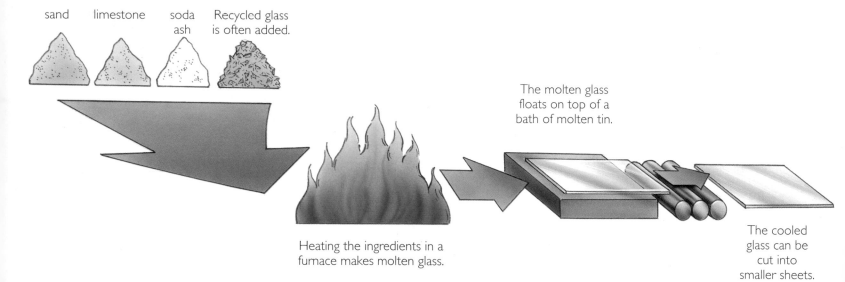

sand   limestone   soda ash   Recycled glass is often added.

Heating the ingredients in a furnace makes molten glass.

The molten glass floats on top of a bath of molten tin.

The cooled glass can be cut into smaller sheets.

HOW IS GLASS BLOWN?

GLASSBLOWERS dip a long tube into molten glass, then blow air into it as it cools, causing the glass to form a bubble. While it is still very warm, this bubble can be shaped, cut with shears, or added to other glass shapes. A slightly different method is used when glassware is made by machine. Then, lumps of hot glass are placed in a mould and air is blown in to force the glass to the sides of the mould. With both methods, the glass can be engraved, or sandblasted to give it a rough texture, after it has cooled.

Sweden is famous for its handblown glass. Here the glassblower is positioning molten glass to be shaped.

The more air that is blown into the glass, the thinner it becomes. Very delicate objects can be made.

HOW ARE STAINED GLASS WINDOWS MADE?

SINCE MEDIEVAL TIMES, glorious decorative windows have been made by joining small pieces of coloured and painted glass together with lead strips. The lead is soft and easy to bend but strong enough to hold the glass.

Stained glass has been popular for centuries. In the days when most people could not read, the stained glass in Christian churches told biblical stories in a way that the congregation could understand. It also meant that no one could look out of the window during lengthy sermons!

HOW WERE WINDOWS MADE BEFORE GLASS WAS WIDELY AVAILABLE?

WINDOWS have three main purposes: to let light into a building, to allow ventilation, and to allow the occupants to see out. Although glass has been made for thousands of years, it is only comparatively recently that techniques have been developed for making large sheets of glass for windows. Before that, although small sheets of glass were available, they were expensive. Small windows were sometimes covered with thin panels of horn. Although this could not be seen through, it did let in a certain amount of light and kept out cold winds.

Buildings dating from the sixteenth century or earlier usually have very small windows, in which little panes of glass can be fitted into wooden frames. Strips of lead may be used to hold them in place.

HOW ARE MIRRORS MADE?

MIRRORS are made by coating the back of a sheet of glass with an alloy of mercury and another metal. This means that light does not pass through the glass, but is bounced back to give a reflection.

As mirrors show us ourselves, they have often been thought of as slightly mysterious, as in the story of Snow White.

This castle has very small windows so that there are few entrances for enemy arrows and bullets. A narrow slit was all that was necessary for the castle's inhabitants to fire on attackers outside. In any case, large windows would have been terribly draughty.

Nowadays we are used to seeing entire buildings covered with glass, but vehicles need windows too. This boat allows tourists an uninterrupted view of Paris, as it travels down the River Seine in France.

fast facts

WHAT IS GLASS FIBRE?

Glass fibre is a material made of glass that is spun into very, very fine fibres. It is used to add strength to some plastics and for insulation. Both heat and sound are unable to pass through it easily.

HOW IS OVENPROOF GLASS MADE?

Glass in which food is cooked needs to be very tough and resistant to rapid changes in temperature. A chemical called boron oxide is added to the glass to give it these properties.

WHAT IS REINFORCED GLASS?

Everyone knows that most glass shatters quite easily, but when glass is used to make a roof, for example, breakage could be extremely dangerous. For this reason, in places where increased security is needed, glass is reinforced by having a mesh of wire embedded in it. Even if the glass breaks, the wire will remain in place and prevent the glass from shattering into large, sharp pieces.

WHEN WAS GLASS FIRST MADE?

Ancient civilizations, such as the Egyptian and Roman Empires, certainly used glass, and glass objects were being made in Mesopotamia 4500 years ago.

HOW IS GLASS RECYCLED?

It is very easy to recycle glass. It is simply broken up and melted, before being shaped again in the normal way.

WHY DO WE COOK FOOD?

There are several reasons why food is cooked. Most obvious is the fact that cooking makes food hot! In cold weather, hot food is especially warming and comforting. Cooking also alters the flavour and texture of food. Heat causes chemical reactions to take place, altering the way that the food tastes and feels in our mouths. Because of these chemical reactions, cooking may also make food easier to digest. Finally, cooking can make food safer to eat by killing bacteria within it.

Preservatives extend the life of foods, so that bacteria do not cause them to deteriorate within days or even hours.

HOW DOES YEAST WORK?

YEAST is a single-celled living organism that digests starches and gives off carbon dioxide gas in the process. Bread can be made light and airy by mixing yeast into the flour and water that make up bread dough. The dough is then left to rise in a warm place. The warmth encourages the yeast to give off tiny bubbles of carbon dioxide, which are trapped within the elastic dough. When the dough is put into the oven, some water evaporates from the flour mixture, and the dough becomes firmer, with the tiny bubbles trapped within it.

In a bakery, huge machines mix and knead the dough. Different kinds of flour are used to make different breads, while flavourings, fats and other ingredients may also be added.

Flavourings and flavour enhancers can intensify natural flavours or provide a cheaper way to flavour food.

WHAT MAKES A CAKE RISE?

IN ORDER for a cake to rise and become light and spongy, air has to be trapped inside the mixture, just as it does in bread. Instead of yeast, most cakes contain a raising agent, such as bicarbonate of soda. When it is heated with flour and liquid, chemical reactions take place to produce little bubbles of carbon dioxide, which are then trapped in the mixture as it becomes firm. Another way of incorporating air into cakes is to whisk eggs before adding them to the mixture. The air is trapped in the egg mixture, which becomes firm as it cooks. This method is used in cakes that do not contain fat.

Uncooked cake mixture is a very thick liquid. As it cooks, bubbles form in it, and it expands. This expansion causes the mixture to move upwards (rise) as the baking tin prevents it from expanding in any other direction. As the cake cooks, it becomes solid, taking on the shape of the container in which it is cooked.

Colourings make foods and drinks more enticing. They may replace the colour lost when food is cooked.

Emulsifiers enable fats to be suspended in tiny globules in liquids.

WHY ARE CHEMICALS ADDED TO FOOD?

WHEN WE READ the lists of ingredients on food packaging, they sometimes sound more like a chemistry lesson than a recipe! Nowadays, food safety regulations and the demand of consumers for products with a reliable taste and texture mean that many different additives are found in some foods.

HOW CAN FOODS BE PRESERVED WITHOUT FREEZING?

BACTERIA that cause food to go bad need certain conditions in which to grow. If they are deprived of those conditions, they may die or be unable to reproduce themselves. One thing that bacteria need is water, so drying foods can help to preserve them. Bacteria cannot reproduce at temperatures below 6°C (39°F) or above 37°C (98°F), so making them hot or cold can prevent them from being active. Canning preserves food by sealing it into a can and then heating it to a high temperature, killing off the bacteria inside. As no more bacteria can enter the can, the food is safe for a long time, until the can is opened. High concentrations of salt or sugar prevent bacteria from being able to use available water, as can acids, so foods such as pickles and preserves are cooked and stored in brine (a mixture of salt and water), vinegar or sugar.

WHAT ARE THE BASIC FOOD FLAVOURS?

MOST OF US can recognize hundreds of different flavours if tested blindfold, but food technologists see these as mixtures of four basic flavours: sweetness, sourness, bitterness and saltiness. Flavour receptors on different parts of the tongue are best at sensing these flavours. You can test this for yourself with a little sugar for sweetness, salt for saltiness, vinegar for sourness and squeezed lemon peel for bitterness, but hold your nose as you test so that aromas do not affect your judgment.

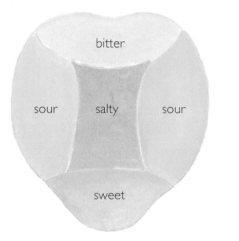

Although our tongues take in taste information, it is our brains that process it.

HOW DOES PACKAGING HELP TO PRESERVE FOOD?

THE MAIN WAY in which packaging helps to preserve food is by preventing bacteria from contaminating its contents, but modern packaging is very sophisticated. Some foods are vacuum packed, so that plastic wrappings exclude any air from the product. Other kinds of packaging are designed to trap gases such as oxygen, nitrogen and carbon dioxide. Mixtures of these help to preserve different foods and to give them a pleasant appearance. Meats, for example, can be kept pink and fresh-looking. Sometimes you will see that meat looks browner where it touches the packaging. This is because the gases cannot reach it at this point. As these are gases that we breathe in every day, they are perfectly safe.

fast facts

DOES FREEZING PREVENT FOODS FROM GOING BAD?

Freezing does not kill the bacteria that cause food to spoil, but it does slow them down so that they are unable to multiply. That means that when a food is defrosted, it will continue to deteriorate at the same rate it would have done if it had not been frozen.

WHAT IS EXTRUSION?

Extrusion is a means of shaping foods by squeezing a mixture through a nozzle and then cooking it quickly so that it retains the shape. Breakfast cereals shaped like hoops or stars are made like this, as is spaghetti and other pasta shapes.

WHAT IS IRRADIATION?

Irradiation is a way of killing the bacteria in food by bombarding it with gamma rays.

WHAT DID LOUIS PASTEUR INVENT?

This French chemist invented a way of making milk safe by heating it. It is not boiled, which would change the flavour, but kept at a high temperature for several minutes. This process is now known as pasteurization.

WHY DO FOODS SOMETIMES SEEM TASTELESS IF YOU HAVE A COLD?

Although we do taste food with the sensitive areas of our tongues, we also use our sense of smell a great deal. Some "flavours" are really aromas. When we have a cold, our sense of smell can be affected, which in turn affects the way our food tastes.

Today's food packaging is often brightly coloured to encourage consumers to buy. But packages also have important nutritional information and a date by which the food should be eaten, while it is still fresh.

WHAT ARE FOSSIL FUELS?

Fossil fuels, which include coal, oil and natural gas, were formed millions of years ago when prehistoric plants and animals died, and their decaying bodies, pressed under layers of rock and earth, became fossilized. Life as we know it would not be possible without fossil fuels. Not only are they burned to supply heat and energy to homes and industry, but by forming the fuel for power stations, they also supply most of the electricity we use. In addition, fossil fuels can be processed to produce many other useful materials, including plastics, dyes and bitumen.

On land, oil is brought up to the surface by a pump called a nodding donkey. It gets its name from the upward and downward motion of its "head"

HOW IS OIL MINED?

THE ROCKS in which deposits of crude (unrefined) oil are found may be hundreds of metres beneath the soil or the sea bed. In either case, a shaft must be drilled down to the deposits. On land, the drill can be set up on a steel structure called a derrick. At sea, a drilling platform is needed. This may have legs that stand on the sea bed or, in very deep water, the drilling platform may float on the surface. Floating platforms must still be anchored firmly to the sea bed so that they can withstand high winds and tempestuous seas.

Helicopters are an oil rig's lifeline, bringing workers, food and supplies.

Some gas from the oil is burnt off on the rig.

Oil rigs need teams of skilled divers to check the drilling platform below the surface and make any necessary repairs.

A pipeline carries crude oil to shore, where it will be refined.

HOW IS OIL REFINED?

CRUDE OIL is refined in a process known as fractional distillation. The oil is heated to about 350°C (660°F) and its vapour is piped into a round column, about 50m (165ft) high. Inside the column, there are perforated trays at different levels. The vapour cools as it rises up the column. Different substances within the crude oil condense at different temperatures (and therefore different levels). They are called fractions.

0°C (32°F)
Fuel gases – methane, ethane, propane and butane – are used to power heaters and lights.

110°C (230°F)
Gasoline compounds include petrol and substances used in the making of plastics, paints and medicines.

180°C (356°F)
Kerosene is used for heating, lighting and as fuel for jet aircraft.

260°C (500°F)
Diesel is used as fuel in large vehicles and some cars.

340°C (644°F)
Residue with more than 20 carbon atoms in each molecule is used for candle wax, heating oil, polishes and bitumen for road surfaces.

crude oil

furnace

---

fast facts

HOW IS OIL FOUND?

Geologists know what kinds of rocks are likely to contain or cover oil deposits. When they find a likely area, on land or at sea, test drilling is carried out to find out if there is oil beneath the surface.

WHAT ARE THE DIFFERENT KINDS OF COAL?

Coal is found in three forms. Lignite, or brown coal, provides the least heat, as it contains less carbon and more water than the other two kinds, which are bituminous coal and anthracite.

HOW ARE OIL RIG FIRES EXTINGUISHED?

If the gas gushing from an oil well is ignited, the fire burns far too fiercely to be put out with water or normal fire extinguishers. Instead, firefighters use a special crane to position an explosive device in the flames. It seems strange to fight a fire with an explosion, but when the explosion occurs, it takes the surrounding oxygen, temporarily depriving the fire and putting it out.

WHY WERE CANARIES TAKEN INTO MINES?

Traditionally, in British mines, a canary in a cage was taken down to the coal face with the miners. The small birds were very sensitive to the dangerous gases that might build up in the shafts. If the canary died suddenly, miners knew that they must run for their lives. Now, the practice seems cruel, but it did save many human lives.

WHAT WAS A DAVY LAMP?

In deep mines, lamps were needed, but naked flames might cause an explosion. In 1815, Humphry Davy invented a safety lamp with a wire mesh around the flame, so that gases would not be ignited.

WHAT IS CRACKING?

CATALYTIC CRACKING is another method of refining crude oil. By applying pressure and heat to some of the heavier fractions obtained by distillation, lighter, more useful fractions are produced.

In an oil refinery, crude oil is separated into usable compounds. By mixing these with other substances and treating them in various ways, literally thousands of useful materials can be made.

WHAT IS PEAT?

PEAT IS partly carbonized vegetable matter, which has decomposed in water. If placed under enormous pressure for millions of years, peat would become coal. Although it does not give off as much heat as coal or oil does when burned, peat is still a useful fuel in some parts of the world, where it is dug from peatbogs. Peat has also been much prized by gardeners for improving the condition of soil.

Peat has been a traditional Irish fuel for centuries. Nowadays, conservationists are concerned that too much digging of peatbogs is destroying the environment that they provide, so alternative fuels and soil conditioners are recommended.

WHICH MINERALS ARE OBTAINED BY MINING?

Strictly speaking, all "minerals" are obtained by mining, as that is one meaning of the word, although it is sometimes used to refer to other inorganic substances. Mining usually involves digging in the Earth's crust, although a few minerals, such as gold, sometimes come to the surface naturally and are found in rivers or on the seashore. Metals, precious and semi-precious stones, and minerals such as sulphur and salt are all obtained by mining.

Rocks found beneath the Earth's surface have many uses in industry. Others, such as malachite, are used for decoration.

WHERE ARE THE WORLD'S MOST IMPORTANT MINING AREAS?

FOR MINING to be economical, minerals need to be found in high concentrations. Sometimes they occur in seams. These are layers of minerals or mineral ores occurring between other rocks. In different parts of the world, rocks dating from various periods of the Earth's history are nearest the surface. This gives mineralogists their first clue as to the minerals that may be found within them.

KEY
☐ precious metals, such as gold, platinum and silver
◇ precious stones, such as diamonds
○ base metals, such as copper, lead, mercury, tin and zinc
■ light metals, such as aluminium, lithium and titanium
▽ rare metals, such as uranium
○ iron, chromium, cobalt, manganese and nickel
▲ industrial minerals, such as asbestos, china clay, mica and talc
△ chemicals, such as borax, nitrates, phosphate, potash, salt and sulphur

IS WATER USEFUL IN MINING?

IN DEEP MINES, water can pose a great danger, undermining layers of rock and causing collapses and flooding, but other types of mining use water to great advantage. Sulphur, for example, can be mined in an unusual process using water. Three pipes of different sizes, one inside another, are drilled into the sulphur reserves. Then extremely hot water, under pressure, is pumped down the outer pipe. This melts the sulphur. Compressed air is then pumped down the central pipe, causing the melted sulphur to move up the middle pipe to the surface. This system was developed by an American engineer, Herman Frasch (1851–1914).

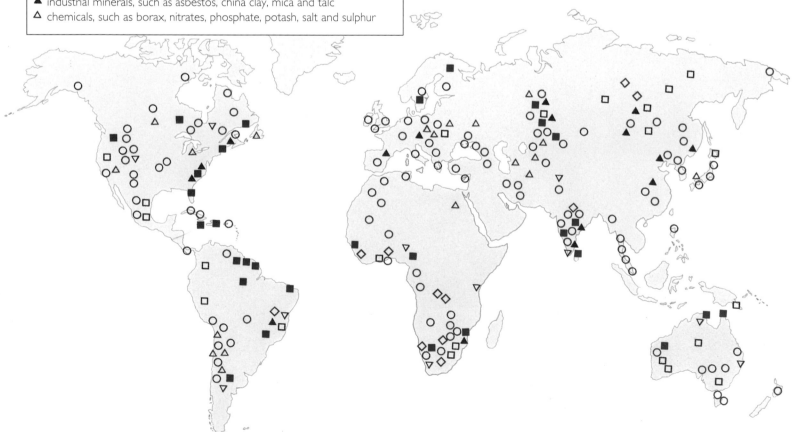

CAN MINERALS BE OBTAINED FROM PLACES OTHER THAN THE EARTH'S CRUST?

FOR PRACTICAL PURPOSES, the Earth's crust is the only source of minerals. There are, of course, huge amounts of minerals in the Earth's core and in space, but at the moment it is not possible for us to reach and use them.

Despite modern safety regulations, mining is still a dangerous occupation. However, opencast mines are less hazardous than deep-shaft mines, where miners have to work hundreds of metres below the surface.

WHAT IS OPENCAST MINING?

OPENCAST MINES are used when the deposit lies near the surface. Overlying earth and rock can be moved by machine or washed away with water. Although opencast mining is cheaper than digging deep mines, some people feel that the environmental costs of it are high, as large areas of land are laid bare and wildlife destroyed. Nowadays great attention is often paid to landscaping the area after an opencast mine has been abandoned. Many are made into parks or wildlife refuges. Planting the areas also helps to stabilize heaps of spoil.

COULD THE EARTH'S MINERALS BE USED UP?

ALTHOUGH there are enormous reserves of iron and aluminium in the Earth's crust, other metals, such as tin, lead, silver, zinc, mercury and platinum are not so plentiful. Some further sources of such metals are known, but at present it would prove too expensive to reach them. As with other non-renewable resources, it is important that we recycle metals or use other materials where possible.

HOW DO UNDERGROUND MINES OPERATE?

DEEP DEPOSITS are reached by driving a shaft vertically into the ground. Miners descend the shaft in a lift. An air shaft takes fresh air down into the mine, where poisonous gases may accumulate. Trucks carry the mined material to a freight lift, which brings them to the surface. Trucks may also be used to take miners to the nearest deposits. Drift mines are dug where the deposit lies in an outcrop of rock near the surface. The seam can be mined directly from the surface, which is often on the slope of a hill.

fast facts

WHAT IS A CARAT?

A carat is a unit of weight for precious stones, equivalent to 200 milligrams (0.007oz). It is also used as a measure of purity of gold. Pure gold is 24 carats.

WHICH IS THE LARGEST DIAMOND EVER FOUND?

A diamond called the *Cullinan* was found in 1905 at the Premier Diamond Mine, in South Africa. It weighed 3106 carats and was cut into 106 polished diamonds.

HOW DEEP IS THE DEEPEST MINE?

A gold mine at Carltonville, in South Africa, has reached a depth of 3581m (11,749ft).

WHICH ARE THE MOST COMMON MINERALS IN THE EARTH'S CRUST?

Aluminium, in the form of the ore bauxite, is the most common mineral in the Earth's crust, followed by iron and magnesium.

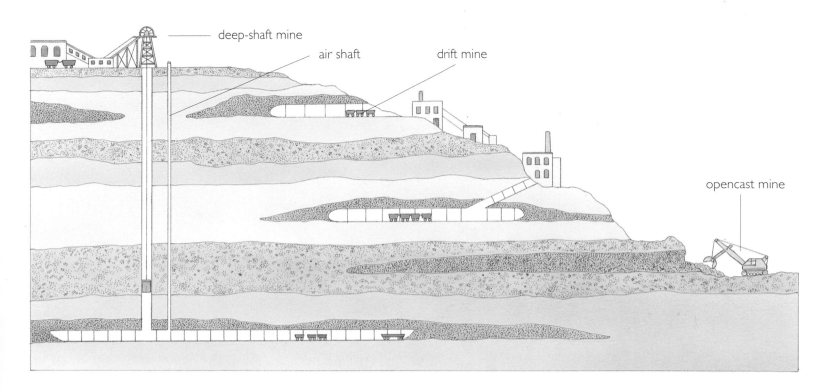

deep-shaft mine
air shaft
drift mine
opencast mine

HOW ARE MODERN MAPS MADE?

A map is similar to an aerial view of the Earth. The landscape is shown as though you are looking down on it, so that the relation of one place to another is clear. But maps are much more than simply bird's-eye views. A great deal of information about the names of places and what they are like can be given in words, numbers and symbols. Although maps are more than aerial snapshots, surveying by plane or satellite has helped mapmakers considerably. Surveying on the ground is time-consuming and may be difficult in remote places. Computer-controlled aerial surveying can give very accurate results and show overall changes in such features as vegetation and coastlines much more clearly than traditional methods.

An aerial view can show roads, rivers, buildings and vegetation, but it cannot tell you the name of a street or the height of a hill. This information has to be added to maps by the mapmakers themselves, known as cartographers.

WHAT IS A PROJECTION?

GLOBES can represent the Earth in miniature, with features shown in a true relationship to each other, but they are not practical to put in your pocket for an afternoon walk. Paper maps are much easier to use, but an adjustment needs to be made in order to show a curved land surface on a flat map. The adjustment chosen is called a projection. Several different projections can be used, depending on the purpose of the map.

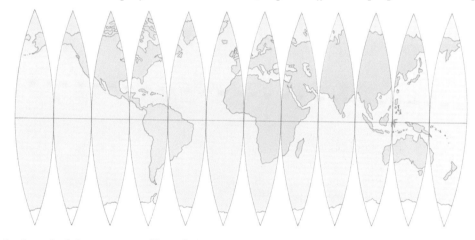

In order to flatten out the Earth's surface, it can be thought of as being divided into segments, like peeling an orange. But that leaves gaps at the top and bottom that make the map impossible to use.

WHO WAS GERARDUS MERCATOR?

GERHARD KREMER (1512–94) was called Gerardus Mercator, meaning merchant, because he made maps for merchants travelling from country to country. In 1569, he made a world map using a projection that has come to be known as Mercator's projection. It is a map that seems familiar to us, but in fact it makes countries at the far north and south of the globe appear much larger than they really are.

This map is based on Mercator's projection, but it does not look very much like the map that he produced in 1569. For one thing, Mercator had no idea of the existence of Australia or New Zealand.

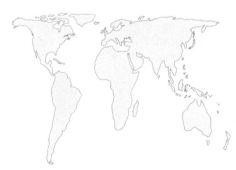

This map of the world is based on Peters' projection. In the 1970s, Arno Peters devised a projection that gave each land mass its true area, but to do so he had to distort the shapes of the oceans and continents.

SCALE : 1:10,000

fast facts

WHAT IS AN ASTRAL MAP?

An astral map is a map of the stars and other heavenly bodies. Astral maps are usually made from the viewpoint of Earth, but still present difficulties as they do not represent a definite surface as maps of the Earth do. The stars are millions and millions of kilometres apart but are shown on maps as though they were merely distant in two dimensions, not three.

WHAT USE ARE OUT-OF-DATE MAPS?

Out-of-date maps are not much use for finding your way today, but they are extremely interesting to historians, who can tell a great deal about the knowledge and interests of the people who made them. Medieval maps of the world, for example, show how much of the Earth was known to European mapmakers at that time. Huge areas of Africa and Asia are left blank, while the Americas and Australasia are not present at all.

WHAT IS A THEODOLITE?

A theodolite is an instrument used by surveyors and mapmakers. It measures horizontal and vertical angles, enabling surveyors to chart the distance between features of the landscape and their relative positions above sea-level.

WHAT IS ORIENTEERING?

Orienteering is a sport that combines map-reading and running. Competitors follow a cross-country course, reaching checkpoints as quickly as possible by using a map. At each checkpoint, there is a rubber stamp, which runners use to show that they have completed all parts of the course.

WHAT IS A KEY?

A MAP must be as easy to read as possible, which means that symbols and colours can often give more information than words. A key explains what the symbols and colours mean, as the one on the right does for the map above.

KEY

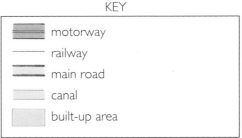

motorway
railway
main road
canal
built-up area

WHAT IS THE SCALE OF A MAP?

MAPS ARE MADE for many purposes. The details that an airline pilot needs to see, for example, are very different from those needed by a person following a local footpath. In addition to the actual content of the map, it needs to be drawn to an appropriate scale. That means that a distance on the map will need to be multiplied by a certain figure to find the distance on the ground itself. On a scale of 1:10,000, for example, one millimetre on the map will be equivalent to 10,000 millimetres (or 10 metres) in real life. The scale of the map above is shown on the map itself.

Many leisure maps for walkers and cyclists are drawn at a scale of 1:50,000.

HOW IS FITNESS MEASURED?

Fitness is the physical condition of an individual. When considered in terms of sports and other physical activity, it is often thought of as having four aspects: endurance, strength, flexibility and speed. Sports differ in the degree to which each of these factors is important. For example, weightlifting requires enormous strength, while a sprinter needs the greatest possible speed. The four aspects of fitness are measured in different ways, but one general way of measuring fitness is to see how the heart responds to physical activity. During exertion, the rate at which the heart beats increases, as it pumps more oxygenated blood around the body. How quickly the heart rate returns to normal after exercise is one way to assess how fit someone is and how exercise is improving their fitness.

Modern exercise bicycles have computers that can give instant readings of the time and distance pedalled and monitor the exerciser's heart rate.

HOW CAN TRAINING IMPROVE PERFORMANCE?

TRAINING improves performance by building up endurance, strength, flexibility and speed. This is done by improving the techniques used in a particular sport, strengthening the muscles used, improving athletes' understanding of how their bodies are performing and giving them confidence to try even harder. There are lots of training methods, and variety can help to prevent boredom setting in.

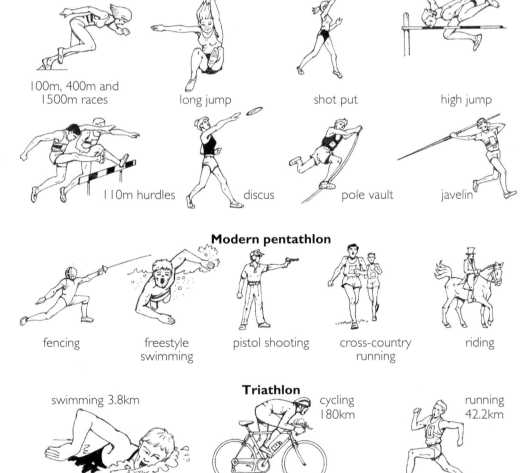

Decathlon

100m, 400m and 1500m races   long jump   shot put   high jump

110m hurdles   discus   pole vault   javelin

Modern pentathlon

fencing   freestyle swimming   pistol shooting   cross-country running   riding

swimming 3.8km   **Triathlon**   cycling 180km   running 42.2km

Many people use weight training to increase their strength. Lifting light weights and repeating the exercise a specified number of times builds muscle strength without creating bulk.

WHAT ARE MULTI-DISCIPLINARY SPORTING EVENTS?

SOME ATHLETES do not specialize in just one sport but maintain a very high standard at several. For them, multi-disciplinary sports, in which points are awarded for performance in a variety of events, are ideal. Some of the most popular are shown above.

HOW ARE RACES ON A CIRCULAR TRACK MADE FAIR?

WHEN ATHLETES are running a circuit, those on the inside tracks have to run less far than those on the outside. In order to ensure that everyone runs the same distance, the start is staggered, so that those on the inside appear to start much further back than those on the outside. It is not until the final straight that it is really possible to see who is winning. Longer races often start from a simple curved line. Athletes break out of their lanes quite quickly and each runs as close to the inside of the track as possible.

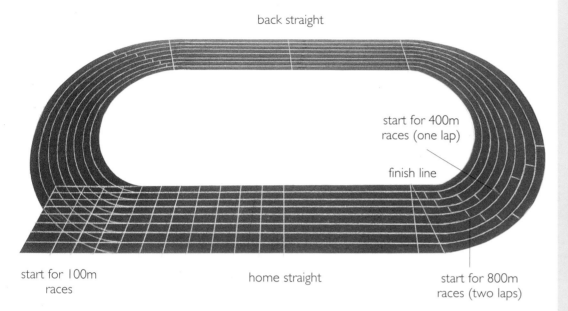

back straight

start for 400m races (one lap)

finish line

start for 100m races

home straight

start for 800m races (two laps)

WHEN WERE THE MODERN OLYMPIC GAMES INTRODUCED?

THE ANCIENT GREEKS held sporting contests over 2000 years ago. In 1896, a Frenchman called Baron Pierre de Coubertin prompted the revival of the Olympic Games. The first modern Olympics were held in Athens, Greece, in honour of their origin. Since then they have been held every four years, except in wartime, in cities all over the globe.

The Olympic flame is a symbol of the Olympic spirit of striving to do one's best. Before each Olympic Games, a series of runners carries the flame from Greece to the site of the Games, where it is used to light the main flame at the opening ceremony.

WHAT ARE THE PARALYMPICS?

IN 1960, in Rome, Italy, the first Paralympics were held. These are Olympic Games for athletes with disabilities. They are now held after each Olympic Games, often on the same site, and give disabled athletes from all over the world an opportunity to compete against each other.

Athletes at the Paralympics train just as hard as their Olympic colleagues. Wheelchairs are specially built for various sports, including track and field events.

fast facts

WHEN WAS THE FIRST MARATHON RUN?

The marathon, a race of 42.195km (26.2 miles), is named after a famous journey by a Greek called Pheidippides, who ran almost that distance to report a Greek victory at the Battle of Marathon in 490BC.

WHAT DOES A SPORTS PHYSIOTHERAPIST DO?

Hard training and harder competition causes many athletes to sustain injuries. A sports physiotherapist uses techniques such as massage, remedial exercises and heat treatment to help the injury to heal properly and quickly.

WHY DO MALE SWIMMERS SHAVE THEIR BODIES?

Competitive swimmers want to move through the water as quickly as possible. Hair may increase the friction between their bodies and the water, so they shave it off. Some even shave their heads!

WHY IS IT IMPORTANT TO WARM UP BEFORE EXERCISE?

Stretching muscles and raising the heart rate before exercise is called warming up. It is important because it helps to prevent injury to muscles and allows the body to enter a higher level of activity gently.

IS SQUASH THE FASTEST BALL GAME?

During a squash match, the rubber ball may travel at over 230km/h (143mph). But in the fast-moving game of pelota (or jai alai), ball speeds of over 300km/h (186mph) have been recorded.

HOW DO GOLF COURSES AND GOLF LINKS DIFFER?

Strictly speaking, links are near to the seashore.

WHAT IS A PLASTIC?

Plastics are polymers, which means that they are made of lots of small molecules joined together to form larger molecules in the form of long chains. Polymers can be manufactured from crude oil, natural gas, or coal. They include artificial fibres and many kinds of plastic. Plastics are extremely useful because they are extraordinarily versatile. They are easy to shape and colour. They can be made into rigid objects or thin, pliable sheets. Some plastics are heatproof, while others melt at low temperatures.

WHAT CAN BE MADE FROM PLASTIC?

ALMOST ANYTHING can be made from plastic! Plastic packaging keeps food fresh and protects it from bacteria. A plastic coating, called Teflon, can prevent food from sticking to cooking pans. Plastic can be elastic, like the skin of a balloon, or very rigid and reinforced with other fibres, as in a protective helmet. Plastic can also be a good insulator. A plastic sleeve on electrical wiring protects the wires from corrosion and the user from electric shocks. Polystyrene packaging can help to keep take-away food warm. Plastic can be dyed in bright colours or completely transparent, to make spectacles and contact lenses. Without plastics, there would be less music in our lives, with no cassette tapes, compact discs or even old-fashioned records.

HOW IS PLASTIC SHAPED?

PLASTIC may be shaped in various ways. It can be extruded (pushed through a nozzle when liquid) to form sheets, tubes and fibres. Molten plastic can be poured into moulds. Vacuum forming is a way of making complicated plastic shapes. A sheet of warm plastic is placed over a mould, then the air is sucked from under it so that the sheet is pulled firmly against the sides of the mould. When the plastic is cooled, it retains the mould's shape. Disposable cups are often made in this way.

WHAT IS THE DIFFERENCE BETWEEN THERMOPLASTICS AND THERMOSETS?

SOME PLASTICS, such as polythene, can be melted and reshaped over and over again. These plastics are recyclable and are called thermoplastics. Other plastics are more resistant to heat and cannot be melted and reshaped. They are known as thermosets. Plastic kitchen worksurfaces and the hard plastic casings around some electrical goods are made from thermosets.

Many inexpensive plastic products are made from fairly flexible thermoplastics, such as polythene. This can be formed in thin sheets or moulded.

The plastic casing of this glue gun is made from thermoset plastic. It needs to be rigid and to resist the heat generated inside it.

ARE THERE ANY NATURAL POLYMERS?

STARCH, rubber, wool, silk and hair are all natural polymers. Their molecular structure, under the right conditions, makes them strong and flexible.

The sap of rubber trees is a white, milky substance called latex. It is collected by cutting the bark and allowing the latex to run into a cup underneath. When heated and treated, the latex solidifies into rubber.

HOW HAVE PLASTICS CHANGED OUR LIVES?

PLASTIC MATERIALS can be shaped very efficiently by machines, so plastic objects are cheaply made in great numbers. Some people think that this has contributed to the "disposable society", where we are inclined to throw something away when it is worn or broken, instead of trying to mend it, as would have happened in the past. They warn, too, that most plastics do not easily decay, so our thrown-away food cartons and shopping bags will remain to pollute the planet for years to come. However, plastics have also brought great benefits, playing a part in so many aspects of our lives that it is difficult now to imagine the world without them.

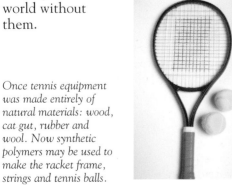

Once tennis equipment was made entirely of natural materials: wood, cat gut, rubber and wool. Now synthetic polymers may be used to make the racket frame, strings and tennis balls.

It was a natural polymer, rubber, that was used to make the first truly waterproof clothing, when Scottish chemist Charles Macintosh (1766–1843) sandwiched a layer of rubber between two pieces of cloth. Today, many different waterproof materials are made from polymers, using plastic coatings and artificial fibres.

WHO BUILT THE FIRST COMPUTER?

In the early 1830s, an English inventor called Charles Babbage (1792–1871) designed the first programmable computer and began to build it. In fact, he never finished, as the machine was extremely complicated! This computer was entirely mechanical. Over a hundred years had to pass before the electronic components that are used today were invented.

monitor

central processing unit (CPU)

keyboard

mouse

WHAT ARE THE MAIN PARTS OF A COMPUTER?

THE CENTRAL PROCESSING UNIT (CPU) is the "brain" of a computer, where its calculations take place. It is contained within a larger processing unit. In order to give instructions to the computer, input devices, such as a keyboard, stylus, mouse, or joystick, are needed. The monitor enables the user to see data on a screen. Many other machines, called peripherals, can also be connected to the computer. They include printers, scanners and modems.

HOW IS INFORMATION STORED IN A COMPUTER?

INSIDE A COMPUTER is a "hard disk", which is able to store information (data) even when the machine is turned off. But there are also two other kinds of storage in a computer. ROM (read-only memory) stores the instructions that tell the computer how to start working when it is first switched on. RAM (random-access memory) stores data that is in use. To make sure that data is permanently stored, it must be "saved" on the hard disk before the computer is switched off.

WHAT IS THE DIFFERENCE BETWEEN HARDWARE AND SOFTWARE?

THE HARDWARE of a computer consists of all the parts described above: the machine itself and any other machinery that is attached to it. But a computer by itself is simply a collection of components. In order to do anything at all, it must be programmed (given a set of instructions). Programs are what is known as software. They are written in a code that a computer can "understand" and act upon. The codes in which programs are written are sometimes called languages.

floppy disk   compact disc   cassette   optical disk

An enormous amount of data can be stored in a computer's memory, but as a back-up and so that data can be shared between machines, several different portable storage devices are used.

230 MB   230

HOW DOES A MOUSE WORK?

A MOUSE is a device for giving the computer information (an input device). When the mouse is pushed around on a mat, a pointer on the computer's screen is moved, indicating how data needs to be changed, moved or processed. Tiny beams of light inside the mouse shine through slotted wheels. The ball of the the mouse moves as it is pushed across the mat, and the beams of light are interrupted in a way that tells the computer the direction that the mouse is moving.

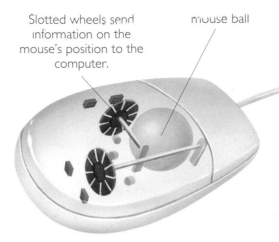

Slotted wheels send information on the mouse's position to the computer.

mouse ball

WHAT IS INSIDE THE PROCESSING UNIT OF A COMPUTER?

INSIDE the processing unit of a computer are collections of integrated circuits (microchips) and other components, usually positioned on circuit boards. There are also slots for floppy disks and CDs to be inserted, a "hard disk" on which data is stored, and perhaps devices such as fans to keep the components cool. Portable computers also have space for a battery, which can be recharged.

Many computers have what are known as expansion slots. Special circuit boards can be inserted into these to increase the computer's power or allow it to perform a particular function.

WHAT IS A PIXEL?

A PIXEL is a tiny dot of colour, which, together with millions of other dots, makes up a picture on a computer or television screen. It is short for "picture element".

fast facts

WHAT DOES CAD STAND FOR?

CAD stands for "computer aided design". There are very few areas of manufacturing and production that do not now call on computers to help with designing new products and improving existing ones.

WHAT DOES THE WORD "COMPUTER" MEAN?

A computer is simply something that can "compute", or calculate. Although today computers can be used for much more than simple calculations, all their functions are based on mathematics.

WHAT IS PROCESSING?

Processing is anything that the computer does to data. It could include sorting it, changing the way it looks, performing calculations on it, or any number of other activities.

WHAT IS A MODEM?

A modem is a device that links a computer to a telephone line or other communication system. It enables information to be shared between computers directly or via the Internet, which is a huge "net" of computer connections stretching across the world.

HOW DO COMPUTERS TODAY DIFFER FROM THE FIRST ELECTRONIC ONES?

Early computers took up whole rooms, which were filled with machinery and spools of whirring magnetic tape. Today, a personal computer (PC) can sit on top of a desk, yet offers many times more power than those huge machines. Today's computers are much faster and have huge memories compared with their ancestors. They are also able to handle pictures and even video footage in a way that was impossible even a few years ago.

HOW DOES AN ELECTRIC MOTOR WORK?

An electric motor uses a current and a magnetic field to create motion. A specially shaped coil of wire, called an armature, is positioned between the poles of a permanent magnet. When an electric current is fed into the wire, the coil becomes a magnet too and forces of attraction and repulsion between it and the permanent magnet cause the armature to move around its axis. A device called a commutator then reverses the current, so that the armature's magnetic poles are reversed and it turns through 180 degrees. If the current is continually reversed, the armature is always turning on its axis. It is this motion that can be used to drive a huge number of machines, such as washing machines, hairdriers and food processors.

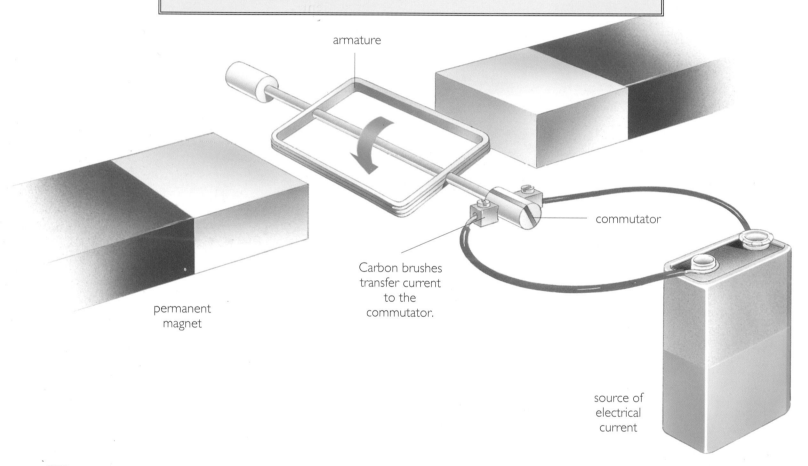

armature

commutator

Carbon brushes transfer current to the commutator.

permanent magnet

source of electrical current

WHAT IS THE LEFT-HAND RULE?

FLEMING'S LEFT-HAND RULE enables you to use your hand to work out the direction of motion of a current-carrying wire in a magnetic field. Hold your hand as in the picture, with the first finger pointing in the direction of the magnetic field and your second finger in the direction of the electric current. Your thumb will now point in the direction of motion of the wire.

WHAT IS THE RIGHT-HAND RULE?

FLEMING'S RIGHT-HAND RULE enables you to tell in which direction a current flows in a wire that is moved in a magnetic field. Hold your hand as shown and point your thumb in the direction of motion and your first finger in the direction of the magnetic field. Your second finger will then point in the direction in which current flows in the wire.

HOW DOES AN ELECTRIC LIGHT WORK?

INSIDE many electric light bulbs is a wire called a filament, made of tungsten. When current is passed through the wire, it glows white hot, giving off light and some heat. As the oxygen has been removed from the bulb, combustion cannot take place, so the wire does not burn out immediately.

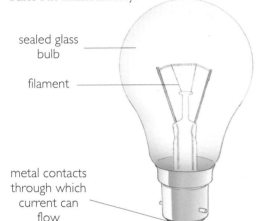

sealed glass bulb

filament

metal contacts through which current can flow

WILL ELECTRICALLY POWERED VEHICLES EVER BE POSSIBLE?

ELECTRICALLY POWERED VEHICLES have been in use for many years! Powering motor cars with electricity does present certain problems, as batteries are heavy and a car's energy requirement is high. This means that the distance an electric car can travel before it is recharged may be too low for many uses. In hot countries, engineers have experimented quite successfully with supplementing a car's battery power with solar power, using solar panels on the roof of the car.

Where vehicles can obtain electrical energy from a fixed wire or track, there is no problem about electrical supply. Electrically powered trains, such as the French train shown above, are the fastest in the world.

We are used to thinking of small domestic electric light bulbs, but in some situations a great deal more light is needed. Some lighthouses have their own generators, which must be kept working all the time if the light is not to fail.

Specially designed electrically powered wheelchairs and vehicles enable disabled people to move about at the same speed as pedestrians.

WHAT IS A GENERATOR?

A GENERATOR is a machine that produces electrical current by moving a wire in a magnetic field. Energy is needed to move the wire. This may come from steam, wind, moving water, or, in the case of the small generator called a dynamo that may be found on some bicycles, from the movement of human legs! Dynamos produce just enough electrical energy to power the lights of a bicycle, but this energy is not stored. If the cyclist stops pedalling, the lights dim and go out.

WHO BUILT THE FIRST ELECTRIC MOTOR?

The first electric motor was based on the work of Michael Faraday (1791–1867), an English physicist. Not only was he the first to show how current and a magnetic field could produce motion, but he also discovered the principle of the generator.

WHAT IS ALTERNATING CURRENT?

Alternating current is electrical current that continually changes direction. This happens many times in a second.

WHAT IS DIRECT CURRENT?

Direct current is electrical current that flows in only one direction.

HOW DOES A FUSE WORK?

A fuse is a short piece of wire, often sealed in a plastic and metal casing, that forms the weakest link in a circuit. If the current in the circuit becomes too high, the fuse wire will melt, breaking the circuit.

WHAT IS A SOLENOID?

A solenoid is another name for a coil of wire in which an electromagnetic field is created when a current passes through it.

The windmills of a wind farm can power generators to produce electricity for hundreds of homes.

WHAT IS A MAGNETIC FIELD?

A magnetic field is the area around a magnet in which its magnetic force operates. A magnetic object that is placed within the field will be attracted or repelled by the magnet. When iron filings (tiny slivers of iron) are placed near a magnet, they line up to show its magnetic field. In fact, each tiny piece of iron has become a small magnet. The mini-magnets show how strongly each part of the large magnet attracts them.

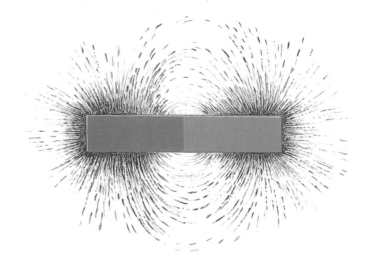

HOW IS AN ELECTROMAGNET MADE?

WHEN AN ELECTRIC CURRENT runs through a wire, it creates a magnetic field. If the wire is wound round and round an iron core, the coil and core become strongly magnetized whenever the current is turned on. The coil of wire is called a solenoid.

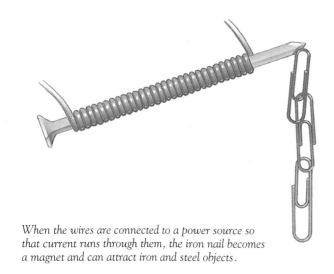

When the wires are connected to a power source so that current runs through them, the iron nail becomes a magnet and can attract iron and steel objects.

HOW DOES A COMPASS WORK?

THE EARTH has a core of molten iron and is itself a huge magnet. Its magnetic field acts as though there were a bar magnet running along the axis of the Earth. A compass contains a magnetized needle, which can turn freely. No matter which direction the compass is facing, the needle will turn to point towards the North Pole. The compass can then be rotated so that its north point lines up with the needle and the other directions can be read.

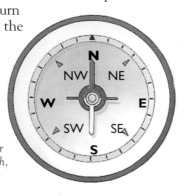

The abbreviations round a compass stand for North, North-East, East, South-East, South, South-West, West and North-East, reading clockwise from the top.

WHAT ARE THE POLES OF A MAGNET?

LIKE THE EARTH itself, each magnet has a north and a south pole. If it can turn freely, the north pole of a magnet will turn towards the North Pole of the Earth. The south pole of a magnet will be attracted towards the South Pole of the Earth. Confusingly, the Earth's North Pole actually has a south magnetic pole, which is why the north pole of a magnet is attracted to it. For the rule is that like poles repel each other (push each other away), while unlike poles attract.

The north and south poles of the two magnets attract each other.

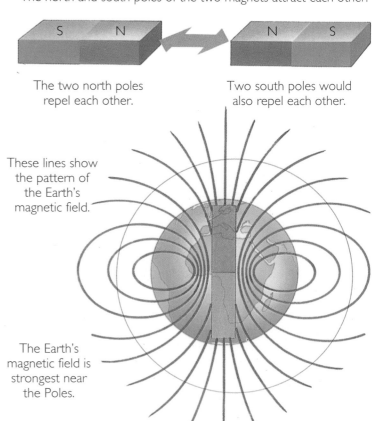

The two north poles repel each other.

Two south poles would also repel each other.

These lines show the pattern of the Earth's magnetic field.

The Earth's magnetic field is strongest near the Poles.

WHAT ADVANTAGES DO ELECTROMAGNETS HAVE OVER ORDINARY MAGNETS?

THE FACT that an electromagnet ceases to become a magnet when the current is turned off can be used to great effect in large and small machines. For example, a powerful magnet can lift very heavy weights of iron and steel in a factory, but that would be no good if the magnet could not be persuaded to release them. With an electromagnet, the current can be stopped and the load released.

An electromagnet can save people who live up several flights of stairs from having to walk down to the front door when the bell rings. They can simply find out who is calling by means of an intercom and then press a switch to let the caller in. The switch turns on a current that activates an electromagnet. The magnet attracts the door latch, pulling it back and allowing the visitor to enter. Then a spring allows the latch to slip back into place.

HOW DOES MAGNETISM CREATE A MAGNIFICENT LIGHT SHOW?

THE EARTH'S North and South Poles attract charged particles from the Sun. Within the atmosphere, these collide with molecules of gas to cause spectacular light shows, called the *aurora borealis* (northern dawn), which can be seen in the Arctic Circle.

When the weather conditions are right, the aurora borealis, also known as the northern lights, can sometimes be seen outside the Arctic Circle in the northern hemisphere.

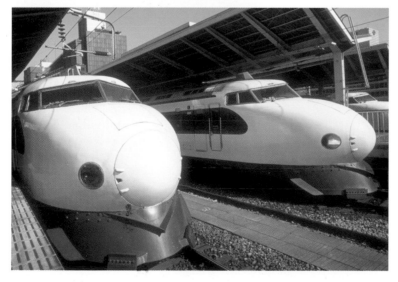

Maglev trains are very quiet for the passengers, as there is no sound of wheels rattling on tracks.

WHERE ARE TRAVELLERS MAGNETICALLY LEVITATED?

IN JAPAN, "maglev" trains run just above, not on, their tracks. Both the bottom of the train and the track itself are magnetic. The magnets repel each other, so the train hovers just above the track, enabling it to run with less friction and so reach higher speeds.

fast facts

WHO DISCOVERED ELECTROMAGNETISM?

Electromagnetism was discovered by a Danish physicist called Hans Christian Oersted. In 1820, he noticed that an electric current could cause a compass needle to deflect. Previously, only magnets had been seen to do this.

HOW CAN MAGNETS HELP WITH RECYCLING?

Before cans used for food and drink are melted down to be recycled, they need to be separated into those made of steel and those made of aluminium. As steel is magnetic but aluminium is not, a huge magnet is held over the pile of cans and the steel ones are picked up by it, leaving the aluminium ones behind.

WHERE DOES THE WORD "MAGNET" COME FROM?

Magnets are so called because the ancient Greeks found magnetic rocks in an area called Magnesia, in what is now Turkey.

WHAT ARE FERROMAGNETIC METALS?

Ferromagnetic metals are those that can be magnetized: iron and steel.

WHAT WAS A LODESTONE?

A lodestone was an early compass, used by sailors to navigate their ships. It was a piece of magnetite, a a rock containing iron, that was naturally magnetic.

CAN MAGNETS WORK THROUGH NON-MAGNETIC MATERIALS?

Depending on its strength and the thickness of the material between it and a magnetic material, a magnet can still work. For example, it can be attracted to a refrigerator door through a piece of paper.

WHAT IS ARABLE FARMING?

Arable farming is the growing and harvesting of crops, particularly where the ground is ploughed between harvests, as the term comes from the Latin word for ploughing. Arable farming is of enormous importance to the world's population, since most of us rely on grains or vegetables for our staple foods.

WHICH ARE THE WORLD'S MOST WIDELY GROWN CROPS?

Wheat is the most widely grown crop, as its various hybrids can grow in a variety of soils and climates. Apart from some grains kept for seed, harvested wheat is ground into flour to make bread, pasta and baked goods.

Rice is the main food for over half the world's population, largely in Asia and South America. Up to three crops of rice per year can be harvested from the same well-watered land. Rice needs a growing-season temperature of over 21°C (70°F).

Maize, or corn, originated from the Americas but is now grown in all warm parts of the world. It is used for human food, as a vegetable, and in the form of maize flour and breakfast cereals. It is also milled and fed to animals.

WHICH CROPS ARE NOT GROWN FOR FOOD?

NOT ALL CROPS are grown for human or animal food. Cotton, flax and jute are grown to be made into fabric. Esparto grass may be cultivated for the manufacture of rope and paper. Tobacco is grown for smoking, while bamboo canes have hundreds of varied uses.

Other non-food crops, such as lavender, are grown for the perfume and cosmetics industries.

1st year — oats, fallow, wheat, turnip

2nd year — potato, oats, fallow, wheat

3rd year — barley, turnip, oats, fallow

4th year — fallow, barley, potato, oats

A typical four-year rotation is shown here. During fallow years, grass or clover was grown. The latter was particularly good for restoring nitrogen to the soil.

WHAT WAS THE AGRICULTURAL REVOLUTION?

IN EUROPE in the Middle Ages, large fields were often divided into strips, with individuals farming their strip as intensively as possible. Since little was understood about the nutrients that plants need and the use of fertilizers, the soil in these strips soon became exhausted, with poorer and poorer yields resulting. The Agricultural Revolution was a change in farming practice that took place gradually during the eighteenth century. The technique of resting ground for a year (leaving it fallow) and rotating crops, so that the same crop was not grown year after year on the same plot, was tested and found to improve harvests. A two-year rotation, and later three- and four-year rotations came to be widely practised.

WHICH ARE THE MOST COMMONLY FARMED ANIMALS?

LIVESTOCK is farmed chiefly to supply foods such as meat, eggs and milk, but also for leather, fur and wool. Animal by-products may also include glue, gelatin and fertilizer. The most commonly farmed animals in the world today are shown below.

Cattle are found all over the world, reared for meat, milk and as draught animals. Cows remain in milk for up to 10 months after the birth of a calf. Different breeds of cattle are suited to almost all climates.

Bred for meat, eggs and feathers, poultry may be chickens, turkeys, ducks or geese. Recently, ostriches have also been farmed. Poultry are often reared indoors for all of their comparatively short lives.

Sheep are kept for meat, milk and wool. They can survive on poorer pasture than cattle. Huge numbers of sheep are raised in Australia and New Zealand, where vast areas of land are given over to them.

There are very few parts of the pig that cannot be used as meat, leather, bristles or fat. Traditionally allowed to roam in woodland, they are now kept in purpose-built huts and intensively farmed.

HOW CAN FISH BE FARMED?

FISHING in the open seas is expensive, dangerous and increasingly difficult as some fish stocks diminish. Fish farming involves using lakes, rivers and netted-off coastal areas to raise fish that can be harvested more easily. Freshwater fish and shellfish have been most success-fully farmed in this way. Many deep-sea fish require conditions that are impossible to recreate in managed waters.

The oceans are so immense that it seems impossible that they could be over-fished, but modern fishing boats are like huge floating factories. They can be at sea for weeks, processing and freezing on board the fish that they literally scoop from the sea. The latest ultrasonic aids help in finding shoals of fish.

HOW HAS MACHINERY CHANGED FARMING?

MACHINERY has made it possible for the work of a dozen farm workers to be done twice as quickly by one worker. There are fewer people working on the land in developed countries than ever before. Machinery exacts a price from the environment as well, as hedges and ditches are removed to allow larger machines to work the enormous fields. Crops have been bred for the machine age, too. They need to ripen together, not over a period of time, so that machinery can harvest them in one operation.

There are still many parts of the world where traditional farming methods are used, but the use of machinery is increasing year by year.

WHO WAS HIPPOCRATES?

*Hippocrates is often described as "the father of modern medicine".
He was a Greek doctor, living in the fourth and fifth centuries BC,
who taught that a doctor's first duty is to his or her patient and that
the aim must at all times be to try to do good rather than harm.
When they qualify, many modern doctors take the Hippocratic
Oath, promising to follow these principles throughout their careers.*

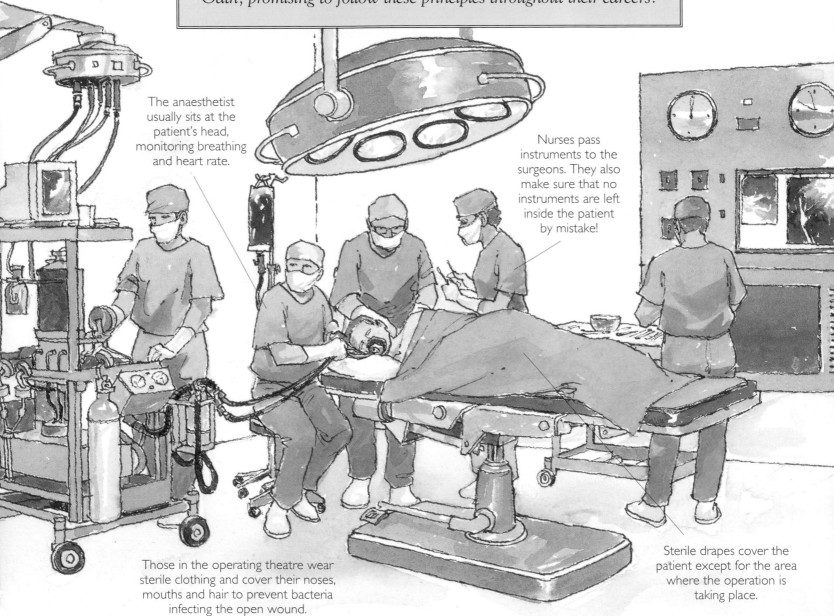

The anaesthetist usually sits at the patient's head, monitoring breathing and heart rate.

Nurses pass instruments to the surgeons. They also make sure that no instruments are left inside the patient by mistake!

Those in the operating theatre wear sterile clothing and cover their noses, mouths and hair to prevent bacteria infecting the open wound.

Sterile drapes cover the patient except for the area where the operation is taking place.

WHAT WAS THE EARLIEST OPERATION?

ARCHAEOLOGISTS have found skulls, dating from at least 10,000 years ago, that have holes drilled into them. Because bone has begun to grow around the holes, they were clearly made while the person was still alive. It is believed that this technique, called trepanning, was the first operation. It was probably done to relieve headaches or to let out evil spirits that were thought to be trapped inside the patient's head.

WHEN WAS ANAESTHESIA FIRST USED?

ANAESTHESIA prevents pain signals from being received by the brain, so that the pain is not felt by the patient. Hundreds of years ago there were few ways to relieve a patient's pain during surgery. Alcohol might be used, but it was not very effective. It was not until the nineteenth century that anaesthetic drugs began to be widely used. The first operation to be performed using a general anaesthetic was by an American surgeon, Crawford Long, in 1842.

fast facts

WHAT IS ACUPUNCTURE?

Acupuncture is an ancient Chinese technique for improving or maintaining health by pushing needles into certain points in the body.

WHAT IS ENDOSCOPY?

Endoscopy is a way of looking inside the body without major surgery. An instrument called an endoscope is inserted into the body through a small hole. Inside it, optical fibres enable the doctor to see internal organs through an eyepiece or on a screen. Endoscopy also enables some operations to be performed using a technique called keyhole surgery, in which only a small incision needs to be made, as the endoscope enables the surgeon to manipulate instruments inside the patient.

HOW DID JOSEPH LISTER HELP TO SAVE LIVES?

Joseph Lister (1827–1912) was an English chemist who introduced the first widely-used antiseptic. By spraying the operating theatre with carbolic acid, he was able to kill harmful bacteria and reduce the infection of wounds dramatically.

WHEN WAS THE FIRST HEART TRANSPLANT?

In 1967, the South African surgeon Christiaan Barnard performed the first transplantation of a heart from a person who had recently died into the body of a man with terminal heart disease. The recipient lived for 18 days. Since then, many patients have lived for years following successful surgery, and the transplantation of other organs, such as kidneys and lungs, is routinely undertaken.

In past centuries, many children did not survive to adulthood. Today, many of the illnesses from which they died can be treated quite easily.

HOW ARE NEW DRUGS DEVELOPED?

RESEARCH CHEMISTS examine different chemicals to find out how they react with other chemicals and with living cells. When a mixture of chemicals is thought to have potential in the treatment of certain conditions, various combinations of the chemicals will be tested to see whether they might be dangerous to living things. Tests on individual cells and on animals are made before human beings are given the new drug. Many people think that drug-testing on animals is wrong, but others feel that this is the best way to make sure that drugs are safe. Trials of the drug, in which some patients are given a placebo (a drug with no active ingredients), are carried out to assess the drug's effectiveness. It is usually only after many years of testing and monitoring that the drug is released for use by doctors.

HOW DO VACCINATIONS WORK?

IN 1796, an English doctor called Edward Jenner (1749–1823) gave the first vaccination. He realized that milkmaids who caught cowpox did not catch the very dangerous disease of smallpox. By injecting the cowpox virus into a child, he was able to vaccinate him against the more serious disease. As the body fights the virus, antibodies are formed in the blood that prevent further infections or infection by some similar viruses. Today, huge vaccination programmes ensure that most children are protected against a range of diseases.

WHAT CAUSES ILLNESS?

UNDERSTANDING the cause of an illness can often help a doctor to bring a patient back to good health or to suggest ways to prevent the illness from recurring or affecting other people. Illness may be caused by an accident, which physically affects part of the body, or it may be brought about by tiny organisms such as bacteria and viruses. Antibiotics are used to treat bacterial infections, while antiviral drugs attack viruses. In both cases, some disease-causing organisms are resistant to drug therapy. Occasionally, the cells of the body seem to act in destructive ways for no obvious reason. This is what happens in some forms of cancer. However, researchers are finding new ways to combat disease all the time.

Drugs in powder form may be pressed into tablets or contained in capsules that dissolve in the stomach. To help pharmacists and patients to distinguish between drugs, they are shaped and coloured in different ways.

Vaccinations are given with hypodermic needles. These are manufactured in sterile conditions and packaged so that bacteria cannot contaminate them.

GLOSSARY

Aerial   A wire or rod that is used to transmit or receive radio waves.

Ballast   Heavy material placed in the hull of a boat or ship to increase its stability.

Book block   The pages of a book, sewn or glued together, before the cover is put onto them.

By-product   A secondary product, resulting from a process mainly designed to extract or manufacture another product.

Cockpit   The place in the fuselage of a plane in which the pilot sits.

Diaphragm   A thin disc or sheet used to separate two areas. The diaphragm is usually designed to vibrate or move up and down when the pressure on one side of it is higher than on the other.

Die   An engraved stamp used for decorating coins and other objects, or a hollow mould for shaping metal or plastic items.

Fuselage   The body of an aeroplane.

Gender   Whether a plant or animal is male or female.

Incision   A cut, such as that made by a surgeon to open the skin for an operation.

Leaf (of a book)   The two sides of a page.

Mica   Any one of several minerals made of aluminium silicate or other silicates with a layered structure.

Organ   Part of the body of an animal or plant that performs a particular function. The lungs, for example, are organs of respiration. The stomach is an organ of digestion.

Piston   A disc or cylinder of metal, wood or plastic that fits closely within a tube and is able to move up and down within it. Pistons create motion in steam and petrol engines.

Receptor   In a living body, a receptor is an organ that is able to sense aspects of the outside world, such as light, heat, aromas and flavours.

Repulsion   The act of repelling: pushing something back or away.

Reservoir   A tank or lake in which large amounts of liquid, especially water, can be stored.

Scanner   A device that can gather information about an image by passing a beam of light across it. Scanners are used to separate colour pictures into four films for printing, and to store an image digitally so that it can be processed and output by a computer.

Spoil   Earth, rocks and minerals brought to the surface during mining but not needed for further processing. Spoil may often be seen piled in heaps near mines and quarries.

Surveying   Determining the nature of a piece of land by measuring distances and angles. Surveys are needed before a new building is constructed and for making maps or finding new deposits of minerals.

Talc   A form of magnesium silicate used, in powdered form, as a lubricant between moving parts or to stop two surfaces from sticking together.

Tempo   The speed of a piece of music, and sometimes its characteristic rhythm as well.

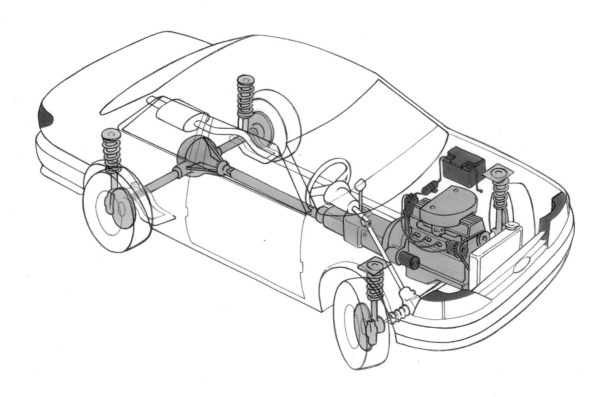

INDEX

· · · · · · · · · · · · · · ·